Date Due

JUL 15 2005			
4/24/14			

Criminal Justice

Recent Scholarship

Edited by
Marilyn McShane and Frank P. Williams III

A Series from LFB Scholarly

Private vs. Public Operation of Juvenile Correctional Facilities

Gaylene Styve Armstrong

LFB Scholarly Publishing LLC
New York 2001

Library of Congress Cataloging-in-Publication Data

Armstrong, Gaylene Styve.
Private vs. public operation of juvenile correctional facilities / Gaylene Styve Armstrong.
p. cm. -- (Criminal justice recent scholarship)
Includes bibliographical references and index.
ISBN 1-931202-00-1 (alk. paper)
1. Juvenile corrections--United States--Evaluation. 2. Juvenile corrections--Contracting out--United States. 3. Privatization--United States. I. Title: Private versus public operation of juvenile correctional facilities. II. Title. III. Series.
HV9104 .A825 2001
365'.42'0973--dc21

2001001750

ISBN 1-931202-00-1

Printed on acid-free 250-year-life paper.

Manufactured in the United States of America.

Table of Contents

List of Tables

List of Figures

CHAPTER 1

Introduction

"There has been almost no systematic empirical research comparing private and government run prisons in terms of quality."

-Charles Logan, 1990

There has been a marked increase in the privatization of correctional facilities during the past thirty years. The placement of juvenile offenders in private correctional programs, such as training centers, boot camps and residential treatment facilities, in lieu of state operated facilities has become common. Currently in the United States, privately operated programs hold more than 39,600 juvenile delinquents under court supervision for a criminally defined offense (Feeley, 1991; U.S. Department of Justice, Office of Juvenile Justice and Delinquency Prevention, 1997). This amounts to 30% of all juveniles under correctional supervision[1]. By comparison, private correctional facilities

[1] Differences in the percentage of the total juvenile offender population varied slightly depending upon the data source. The 1997 Children in Custody Census (U.S. DOJ, OJJDP, 1999) utilized aggregate data from facilities. This census suggested 33% of juveniles were in private facilities. The 1997 Census of Juveniles in Residential Placement (U.S. DOJ, 1999) was based on a biennial census of facilities that collected information on the number of juveniles held and the reason for custody. The CJRP suggested 27.8% of juvenile offenders were in private facilities in 1997.

held only 10.2% of the total adult correctional facility population at year-end 1998 (Logan, 1999; Thomas, 1999; U.S. Bureau of Justice Statistics, 1999).

The expanding role of the private sector in operating correctional facilities this past decade has prompted extensive debate regarding the feasibility of private facilities as a response to the dramatic increase of the offender population. The majority of debates and empirical ventures have focused on the economic aspects of the privatization (Hodges, 1997; McDonald, 1990; Pratt & Maahs, 1999; U.S. General Accounting Office, 1991). Shichor and Sechrest (1995) asserted "the major claim [in favor of privatization] is that private companies following the profit motive can perform most services cheaper and more effectively than can the public sector, which is considered to be unmotivated, ineffective, and unresponsive to the public's needs and demands" (p. 457).

Scholars have also debated philosophical and organizational issues related to private correctional facilities. A limited number of researchers have explored the environmental quality of conditions of confinement in private adult correctional facilities (Logan, 1992) as well as the recidivism rates of private facilities as compared to public facilities (Clinton, Stolzenberg, & D'Alessio, 1997; Lanza-Kaduce, Parker & Thomas, 1999). I will provide an in-depth description of these and other issues surrounding correctional facility privatization in the subsequent chapter.

Studies completed in adult correctional facilities have provided the foundation on which many of the debates and tentative conclusions about the effects of privatization rest. This focus within adult facilities is attributable to the recent and dramatic growth of private correctional facilities holding adult offenders. While the capacity of private juvenile correctional facilities has experienced a mere 9% increase between 1991 and 1997, the capacity of private secure adult correctional facilities has increased a dramatic 856% between 1991 and 1998. Although there hasn't been a marked rise in the rate of privatization within the juvenile correctional system, private facilities currently hold one third of all juvenile delinquents. This proportion is much higher than the proportion of adult offenders held in private facilities (30% versus 10%).

Despite the large proportion of juvenile delinquents that are held in private facilities the research on the impact of privatization on juvenile correctional facilities is limited. One reason for this exclusion may be that private correctional facilities for juveniles have existed since the inception of juvenile facilities while the trend toward privatization in adult facilities is much more recent.

Another reason may be that subtle differences exist between the populations held in adult and juvenile facilities. Historically, private facilities for juveniles have held individuals who are committed for non-criminal activities such as neglect or dependency, in the same facilities as individuals who are committed for criminal offenses. As a result of these mixed populations, researchers examining correctional programs may not have viewed these juvenile facilities as a viable subject of study. However, since 1991 private juvenile facilities have seen a drop in both the proportion and number of these non-offenders (U.S. DOJ, OJJDP, 1997) and have become facilities that hold delinquent-only populations. This study focuses on this latter type of correctional facility.

A final reason that private juvenile facilities have not received the same amount of attention in the literature as received by private adult facilities may be due to media attention and court orders pertaining to the overcrowded conditions within adult facilities. Blakely and Bumphus (1996) pointed out that the magnitude of correctional facility overcrowding in the adult system was such an extensive problem that in 1990, one-fifth of all state correctional facilities were under court order to reduce their populations. The effects of overcrowding were felt primarily in the decreased environmental quality of the facilities. This led the public to have concerns about the safety and ethical treatment of offenders. At present, overcrowding is still a problem in adult facilities.

At year-end 1998, federal correctional facilities were operating 27% above capacity and state correctional facilities were operating between 13 and 22% above capacity (U.S. D.O.J., B.J.S., 1999).

Crowding in juvenile facilities is also evident but has not received equivalent media attention. The juvenile population has continued to increase in the last decade (Howell, Krisberg, Hawkins & Wilson, 1995) evidenced by a 25% increase in the capacity of detention centers and a 73% increase in the average daily population between 1984 and 1994 (Wordes & Jones, 1998). Consequently, over half of the juveniles who were admitted to detention centers in 1995 were admitted to some facility that was already experiencing overcrowding.

Further, adult offenders have been more vocal than juvenile delinquents regarding their overcrowded living conditions as demonstrated by the number of law suits filed against the government by adult offenders because of the poor quality of conditions of confinement in the correctional facilities. However, there have been instances of class action suits brought on the behalf of juvenile delinquents that challenge the inadequate conditions in juvenile facilities (Butterfield, 1998; Demchak, 1989).

Regardless of the reason for the lack of research on the impact of privatization on juvenile correctional facilities, if criminologists and criminal justice practitioners are truly concerned with investigating the overall effects of privatization, inquiry should not be limited to adult facilities but also extended to private juvenile facilities. This study assesses the implications of privatization in juvenile corrections through the examination of the environmental quality of conditions of confinement in both public and private juvenile correctional facilities.

Privatization in this study refers to the process wherein the state continues to fund the costs of incarceration of delinquents but the private sector provides the custodial and programmatic managerial services (Harding, 1997). The juvenile facilities that I will examine herein are residential correctional facilities for juveniles who are incarcerated for committing a legally defined offense. All of the facilities that I will study have met the criteria for a residential facility for juvenile placement as outlined by the Office of Juvenile Justice and Delinquency Prevention (OJJDP) in the Census of Juveniles in Residential Placement. These criteria state that the resident must be (1) less than 21; (2) assigned a bed in a public or private residential facility; (3) charged with or court-adjudicated for an offense; and (4) placed at the facility as a result of the offense. This study will not examine facilities that house juveniles for reasons other than commitment for a legally defined offense. With these criteria in place, the findings will be comparable with studies of quality of conditions of confinement compiled within adult correctional facilities.

This research will utilize data collected from 48 juvenile correctional facilities throughout the United States. These data pertain to the quality of conditions of confinement as perceived by juvenile delinquents (n = 4,590), correctional staff (n = 1,362), and facility administrators (n = 48). I will use these data to ascertain differences in the perceptions of the conditions of confinement by both juvenile delinquents and staff. As well, I will examine the effects of privatization on the adjustment of the juvenile delinquents and the work experiences of the correctional staff.

This study begins by providing the reader with a historical synopsis of the role of the private sector within the adult correctional system wherein the majority of the historical descriptions of the private sector exist. I contrast this synopsis with the historical role of the private sector in the juvenile correctional system. Subsequently, I outline the debates and issues surrounding correctional facility privatization as argued by supporters and opponents.

In the final chapter of the literature review, I discuss the measurement structure that I will use to examine the quality of the juvenile correctional environment. Specifically, I discuss various conditions of confinement models that researchers have developed and in some instances empirically tested within the literature. Researchers have already utilized some of these models, such as Logan's Prison Quality Index, in comparisons of the environment between private and public correctional facilities. Subsequent to the review of the literature, I will outline the present study including the specific research questions examined. I also describe the rationale, instrumentation and methodology used in the collection of the data. Further, I describe the analytical models used and specify the data analysis completed.

CHAPTER 2

Privatization of Correctional Facilities

Privatization of correctional facilities is an important issue on the political agendas of several countries around the globe. The United States already has more than 164 private correctional facilities operated by more than fourteen major corporations such as Corrections Corporations of America (CCA) and Wackenhut. In total, these private correctional facilities held more than 138,243 offenders in 1998 (Logan, 1999). Other countries have studied the development of the American model of privatization that began in the mid 1980s and follow its example. It was the American model that led the United Kingdom to adopt of a limited number of private correctional facilities (Ryan, 1993). Also, in the Australian the state of Queensland, at least one private correctional facility is in place and New South Wales is actively considering the construction of others (McDonald, 1990). At the end of 1995, six contracts for secure adult correctional facilities existed in the United Kingdom and Australia (Thomas & Bolinger, 1996).

In addition to contracting out the entire facility to private entrepreneurs, various criminal justice systems have also contracted out for specific services such as food or medical services. A study by Camp and Camp (1984) discovered that correctional facilities in the United States utilized more than 30 different types of private services that provided more than $300 million annually to the private sector. Additionally, the private sector has more recently provided other private community correctional services such as home detention monitoring, electronic monitoring, pretrial diversion programs, and supervising community service sentences.

Scholars have not questioned and criticized the provision of specific services to the same extent as the fully privatized correctional facilities. One reason for the lack of critiques may be because contracting for a specific service does not challenge the state's authority over the offenders (McDonald, 1990). Further, the private sector has been extensively involved in serving other types of institutionalized populations with limited debate arising. As McDonald (1990) reported, some of these other types of privatized facilities have included psychiatric hospitals (the private sector operates 60%), nursing homes (the private sector operates 92%) and residential drug treatment programs (the private sector operates 75%). The difference in serving these alternative populations is that they serve individual clients' needs as opposed to fulfilling the state's authoritative role in mandatory confinement of a criminal population. At present, the greatest debate surrounding privatization is the contracting of correctional facilities, in their entirety, to private corporations.

The current debates evident within the criminological literature are not as new as one might expect. In fact, the issue of privatization of correctional facilities dates back to the 1800s with the formation of correctional facilities in both the adult and juvenile systems. To fully understand debate and to understand where the future of privatization may lie, this review will explore the history of privatization. In the next few sections of this chapter, I will discuss the history of correctional facility privatization in both the juvenile and the adult correctional systems. This chapter will conclude with an outline of the issues and debates surrounding the utilization of private correctional facilities, some of which have resurfaced from the nineteenth century.

The History of Privatization in the Adult Correctional System

Although the privatization of correctional facilities may appear to be a relatively new idea in the penal system, correctional facility management by the private sector has existed since the days of Jeremy Bentham, circa 1787 (DiPiano, 1991). Since the existence of correctional facilities, the government has allowed private entrepreneurs, during certain time periods, to utilize offenders for their labor in order to assist the criminal justice system in meeting the expenses of housing offenders.

Kentucky was one of the first states to rely on a private contractor to operate the entire correctional facility system. Feeley (1991) suggested that the frustration of high operating costs of the correctional facility led the state of Kentucky to consider privatization. Consequently, in 1825, the state of Kentucky enacted legislation that allowed for the leasing of the entire correctional facility and its population to a private entrepreneur. Kentucky's leasing system survived until the 1880s and subsequently served as a role model for other states such as Tennessee which utilized convict labor in coal mines, manufacturing, and road and railway construction.

California also turned to private entrepreneurs to manage their correctional facilities in the 1850s when the correctional facility capacity increased beyond the state's control. The rapid influx of residents into California at the outset of the gold rush led to California's demand for increased correctional facility capacity. As a solution, private entrepreneurs housed convicts in surplus ships located in the San Francisco Bay and further built and operated the San Quentin penitentiary (Feeley, 1991).

The majority of the southern United States followed the examples set by Kentucky and California toward the end of the civil war (McKelvey, 1977). The southern states' loss in the civil war resulted in the devastation of their economy and the abolition of slavery. The

South's loss further led to a widespread reliance on criminal sanction and convict labor to serve as a means to "control" the black population (Feeley, 1991). The resulting increase in the number of criminal offenders forced the southern states to lease offender labor in all eleven states of the former Confederacy to assist with their operating costs.

Despite numerous claims of offender abuse and poor working and living conditions in most privately operated facilities, the government did not abolish the leasing of offenders and operation of correctional facilities by private entrepreneurs until the early part of the twentieth century (Ethridge & Marquart, 1993). Several factors led up to the eventual demise of private correctional facilities. First, a coalition of citizens in labor, manufacturing and farming industries successfully lobbied for legislation that restricted the use of convict labor and the sale of convict-made goods. The coalition's platform was based on arguments that contract and convict lease systems provided unfair competition. Secondly, reformers successfully mobilized public opposition against the "scandalous" conditions of confinement in the private correctional facility system. Finally, the growth of the modern welfare state increased the government's ability to manage large-scale facilities such as correctional facilities (Feeley, 1991).

The Re emergence of Adult Private Correctional Facilities

The re-emergence of private correctional facilities in the United States in the last few decades has been primarily as a response to the explosion of the offender population. An impressively stable incarceration rate characterized the fifty-year period from the early 1920's to the 1960's averaging 110 offenders per 100,000 members of the general population. This stability was attributable to a homoeostatic process in which incarceration policy was within the control of the functionaries in the criminal justice system. Judges and parole authorities could generally modify their decision to account for overcrowded correctional facilities. However, by 1996 the incarceration rate had increased to 615 offenders per 100,000 members of the general population which was more than five and a half times the rate that had prevailed until the early seventies (U.S. D.O.J., B.J.S., 1997). The dramatic growth of the offender population resulted in seriously overcrowded correctional facilities. By year-end 1998, state correctional facilities operated between 13% and 22% above capacity while federal correctional facilities operated at 27% above capacity (U.S. D.O.J., B.J.S., 1999).

Coinciding with the increase in the offender population since the 1970s, there has been a rapid expansion of correctional facilities. This rapid expansion has resulted in an enormous opportunity for private correctional facilities to develop and grow. Recently, supporters of privatization have touted private correctional facilities as a solution for overcrowding because they view the facilities as a quick and cost-effective means to assist in decreasing overcrowding in the correctional facilities (Ryan, 1993).

Various countries have created the majority of the private correctional facilities through the construction of new facilities as opposed to a take over of existing facilities. For example, in the United Kingdom only one correctional facility to date has gone out for tender to the private sector (Ryan, 1993) but they have built more than five new private facilities in the last decade.

Expansion of new facilities through the private sector has allowed state governments to bypass the taxpayer who the government normally calls upon to bear the capital cost of building new facilities. As a result, the new facilities require less administrative effort and this has expedited their construction time (Logan, 1992). It is through the ability of the private sector to respond quickly and with reduced construction time that private supporters have that expected correctional facilities to assist with overcrowding and thus proliferated. However, the private correctional facilities have not developed without public debate and concern, especially with researchers and practitioners in the public sector who have taken issue with this expansion.

The History of Privatization in Juvenile Correctional Facilities

As I have discussed, the private sector has demonstrated involvement in the adult system in the early 1800s. The government abolished the sector's involvement in the late 1800s but they became subsequently re-involved in the late 1900s. By comparison, the private sector has played a consistent role in both responding to the growth of the juvenile population and in the fundamental development of the juvenile correctional facilities.

If authorities didn't return juvenile delinquents and neglected children to their home in the early 1800s, they confined them within the walls of adult correctional facilities. Historians have described the conditions of the adult correctional facilities during this time period as horribly punitive and inhumane. It was as a result of these deleterious conditions that a separate and distinct juvenile court and juvenile correctional facilities evolved (Seigel & Senna, 1996).

The New York House of Refuge was the first juvenile correctional facility to be established in 1825 by a religious philanthropic organization known as the Society for the Reformation of Juvenile Delinquents (Bernard, 1992). The organization established the facility for children who were in danger of growing up to be "paupers and criminals." Both private entrepreneurs and public authorities implemented the House of Refuge model in a number of other urban areas in the following decade though these subsequent facilities varied widely in their philosophies, design and security levels.

The most significant growth in the development of public juvenile facilities occurred in the second half of the 19th century during the era of reform schools (Krisberg, 1995). During this time, states and private entrepreneurs began to establish reform schools and occasionally they worked in conjunction to operate facilities. The first state reform school, the Lyman School for Boys in Massachusetts, opened its doors in 1846. By 1876, 51 reform schools and houses of refuge were in operation nationwide. The state or local government operated nearly three-quarters of these facilities. By 1890, almost every state outside the South had developed a reform school (Krisberg, 1995). The states based the philosophical foundation of the majority of the schools in a punitive model, attempting to rehabilitate offenders through hard work and discipline.

In the latter part of the nineteenth century, the emphasis of juvenile corrections shifted away from massive housing efforts of the reform schools. Advocates, known as "the child savers," criticized the reform schools and argued that the greater the length of confinement for juvenile offenders in reform school, the less likely that the schools would rehabilitate the youth. This group of advocates, headed by Charles Loring Brace, began an alternative strategy of placing urban youth in apprenticeships with farm families throughout the country. They believed that the agricultural experience would assist in the reformation of the juvenile offenders. This system of placement became known as the cottage system (Bartollas, 1997). Reformers designed the cottages to reflect a home like atmosphere, including having cottage parents, which they postulated to be conducive to rehabilitation. Similar to reform schools, both the private and public sectors operated cottage systems.

The rise of the Civil War greatly affected juvenile facilities by physically destroying many of the reform schools in the South. Further, the inflation rates reduced the available funds used to maintain the correctional facilities and as a result the conditions in juvenile correctional facilities rapidly deteriorated. As a solution to this economic shortage, facilities began contracting out the labor of juvenile delinquents to private entrepreneurs with the aim of increasing the available revenue for juvenile correctional facilities.

The reports of cruel and vicious treatment that existed in the adult facilities became true of the facilities that held juvenile laborers. As a result, the child savers and religious groups criticized the contracting actions of the facilities, calling for states to investigate both public and private juvenile correctional facilities. The result of the investigation was the uncovering of horrid conditions, corruption and abusive practices (Krisberg, 1995) as well as the establishment of the National Prison Association. Unlike the adult system that ended in the total abolishment of private contracting, activists made minimal progress despite reports of negative treatment within juvenile correctional facilities. Both private and public facilities continued to proliferate, housing increased numbers of juveniles. In 1880, there were 11,468 juvenile delinquents in correctional facilities and this number rose rapidly in the next two decades to reach 23,034 juveniles by 1904 (United States Department of Justice, 1986).

With the influence of World War I, correctional facilities began to adopt a militaristic approach to discipline. As Bartollas (1997) described, "living units became barracks, cottage groups became companies, house fathers became captains, and, superintendents became majors or colonels. Military-style uniforms became standard" (p.617). Further, this era experienced the introduction of physical exercise, special massage and nutritional regimens into the daily schedule under the belief that the neglect of the body led to the depraved behavior of the juveniles (Krisberg, 1995). This change in correctional philosophy and the increased number of juvenile delinquents gave rise to the multiplicity of public and privately operated programs including forestry camps, ranches and vocational schools that are evident today.

Today, there are approximately 1,100 public and 2,200 private juvenile facilities in operation (U.S. DOJ, OJJDP, 1995) holding more than 100,000 juvenile offenders. In a 1990 survey of all 50 states and the District of Columbia, Levinson and Taylor (1991) found almost 90% of the jurisdictions had at least one contract with a nonprofit private corporation, 60% contracted with a for-profit organization and another 65% had personal service contracts with private companies. The authors of the study concluded that based on "the responses of 50 jurisdictions, an increasing number of states' juvenile agencies are using the private sector" (p. 248).

The majority of the private and public juvenile facilities are small, non-secure facilities holding a limited number of offenders reminiscent of the cottage system. However, at least 70 facilities house more than 200 juveniles and while only 20% of the private facilities are high security, about 80% of the public facilities are "closed" and secure facilities (Bartollas, 1997).

When compared to the training schools at the turn of the century, the facility administrators have been able to improve the physical conditions of these juvenile correctional facilities, but conditions still vary widely between facilities. Researchers have described conditions of confinement in some facilities as horrendous and health officials have cited facilities for violations such as pollution by vermin, rodents and asbestos (Breed & Krisberg, 1986). Krisberg (1995) suggested the severe conditions of crowding faced by juvenile facilities and, "as a result of increasing caseloads and restricted budgets, many juvenile correctional facilities have experienced deteriorating conditions of confinement and basic lapses in meeting professional standards" (p. 154).

In conclusion, private and public juvenile correctional facilities have coexisted since the original inception of juvenile facilities. As variations of the houses of refuge were developed in various states, private entrepreneurial versions quickly followed. As the juvenile delinquent population expanded, the number of public and private facilities grew to accommodate their rising numbers. It is because of these historical parallels of their development and growth, which I do not expect to find significant differences between the environments of the public and private juvenile correctional facilities that exist today.

Issues and Concerns in the Privatization Debate

The rapid growth of private correctional facilities within the adult system and the sustained large proportion of private juvenile facilities has led to debates about the utility of privatization of correctional facilities. In turn, these discussions have led to a number of perspectives from which private and public correctional facilities can be examined and compared including legal, philosophical, organizational, economic and environmental quality perspectives (Ogle, 1999; Shichor & Sechrest, 1995).

Researchers who have examined the legal implications of privatization have focused on the legal liability of private corporations and the enabling legislation that various states have enacted to regulate the authority of the private facilities over the offenders. Debates about privatization from a philosophical perspective have addressed whether it is appropriate for private corporations to administer punishment to citizens in the place of governmental authorities. Researchers who have debated organizational issues surrounding private correctional facilities have discussed the conflicting goals that are held by private facilities that must both attain a strong profit margin, yet maintain the legitimacy of an institutional environment. Economic debates have focused on the cost-effectiveness of private facilities as compared to public facilities. Lastly, researchers who have debated the potential for differences in environmental quality between private and public facilities have discussed conditions of confinement and population composition. In this next section, I will provide greater detail on each of the areas of debate.

Legal. Legal debates on privatization have focused on two primary issues: (1) the designation of legal liability between the government and the contracted private companies, and, (2) the constitutionality of the state contracting its policing powers to private companies. As Ethridge and Marquart (1993) have discussed, the people have already tested the liability of the government in a civil right lawsuit in *Medina V. O'Neil* (1984). This case was based on the accidental death of a detainee who was in a privately operated correctional facility that held undocumented aliens for the United States Immigration and Naturalization Service (INS). During an escape attempt by several detainees from the correctional facility, a correctional officer accidentally killed one of the detainees. The family of the detainee brought the case to the Federal District Court who ruled that the actions of the correctional officer, whom the private corporation employed, constituted "state action" under 42 U.S.C. Section 1983. Consequently, it was determined that the family could file a wrongful death suit against either the private company or the government (in this case the federal government). Thus, the *Medina* ruling demonstrated that the laws did not immunize the government from liability even when the incarceration services were contracted to private corporations.

To further address concerns of constitutionality and the limits of authority of the private sector, states have developed legislation. This type of legislation, broadly categorized as enabling legislation, consists of standards that have regulated the awarding of contracts to the private sector and attempted to maintain control over private corporations. Recent figures have suggested that at least twenty-one states have created enabling legislation directed toward private correctional operations. Blakely and Bumphus (1996) completed a detailed review of enabling legislation in all twenty-one states. They found enabling legislation generally addressed mandated requirements that any corporation vying for a contract with the state correctional department must meet. They categorized the most frequently mandated state requirements into four categories: contractor qualifications, operational services, treatment services, and the limits of the contractor's authority.

Contractor qualifications addressed the prior experience of the contractor, its history of successful compliance with state requirements and court mandates, accreditation, liability protections, financial stability and the evidence of capital savings to the state. Operational services that the legislation frequently required included were health and medical care, food services, mail/telephone/visitor accommodations, access to legal services and sanitation. Required treatment services included vocational training, educational programs, counseling, mental health programs, and chemical dependency counseling. Finally, enabling legislation frequently stipulated that the state would not delegate certain authorities to private companies. These authorities included calculating offender release and parole eligibility dates, awarding sentence credits and approving offenders for furlough and work release.

Although enabling legislation may not completely alleviate the concerns of those in opposition to private correctional facilities, it does attempt to delineate the state's authority over the offenders in private facilities. Further, setting and maintaining the standards for private contractors will assist the states in avoiding civil law suits in the future. Despite the legislation, many opponents maintain an anti-privatization position based on philosophical grounds against the fundamental nature of the dispensation of punishment by a non-governmental body.

Philosophical. Philosophical debates about privatization have focused on varying punishment ideologies that have questioned whether punishment by private companies is symbolically similar to punishment by the state (DiIulio, 1988). Critics have asked whether it is "proper" for anyone but the state to deprive people of their freedom (DiIulio, 1988; Robbins, 1986). Supporters have suggested that law and civil status binds both the public and the private sector and as such should not be considered to be a significant factor.

Opponents to privatization believe that punishment is one of the core functions of government and only governmental agencies should administer it (DiIulio, 1988). DiIulio asserted "to remain legitimate and morally significant, the authority to govern behind bars, to deprive citizens of their liberty, to coerce (and even kill) them, must remain in the hands of government authorities" (p. 79-80). Further, he suggested that employing the force of community through private correctional facility management undermines the moral writ of the community itself (DiIulio, 1991). In summary, the primary philosophical argument against privatization is that contracting for imprisonment involves an improper delegation of coercive power and authority to private hands (Logan, 1990).

Others have argued that the pertinent philosophical question is whether duly authorized punishment is any more or less legitimate when administered by government employees, as opposed to contracted agents (Logan, 1990). Logan argued that the government does not own the authority to punish. The authority originated in the people and the people delegate it to the government who administers it in trust, on the behalf of the people and subject to the rule of law. He concluded that law binds both state and private actors, and it is the law, not the civil status of the actor that determines legitimacy. Supporters of privatization have also suggested that contracting of facilities in conjunction with government monitoring will add a new layer of independent review of correctional decisions and actions, and thereby improve due process.

Organizational. The recent discussion based on the organizational behavior of private correctional facilities has not been an argument of whether public or private correctional facilities are preferable. Instead, scholars have oriented the discussion to be more theoretical, focusing on organizational adaptations to environmental conflict and on estimating the survival of private facilities through an organizational behavior framework.

Ogle (1999) has suggested profit-seeking private correctional facilities are engaged in an "environmental catch-22" since they must interact with both the institutional environment of corrections and the technical environment of the competitive business market. The organizations must conform to elaborate rules and requirements within the institutional environments if they wish to receive legitimacy and support (Scott, 1992). The correctional organization, Ogle (1999) noted, has served a set of intangible goals that have come to represent and maintain our belief system about criminal behavior and its correction. Further, from a legitimacy perspective the process of correction has been more important than the evaluation of the results. Ogle also suggested "the political, social and legal requirements and expectations for humaneness and fairness in that process [of correction] are quite high regardless of the technical outcomes. Thus legitimacy is more important for organizational survival than is any cost-benefit analysis" (p. 585).

Private correctional facilities must be concerned with maintaining their legitimacy status by adhering to the political, social and legal requirements and expectations for humaneness and fairness. However, private correctional facilities also face the additional charge of addressing the technical environment in which they exist (Ogle, 1999). Scott (1992) defined technical environments as those in which "organizations produce a product or service that is exchanged in a market such that they are rewarded for effective and efficient performance" (p.132). In addition to maintaining legitimacy within society, private correctional facilities must also maintain allegiance to their competitive market, specifically, their investors and their profit margin. Different from the public sector, the institutional environment encapsulates private correctional facilities who are attempting to achieve or maintain a public perception of legitimacy, while also participating in the technical environment which focuses on cost-effectiveness. Ogle (1999) has described this placement as an "environmental catch-22" because corporations design private correctional facilities to create technical efficiency for market survival. However, this design conflicts with the institutionalized environment of corrections. Ogle also suggested that private correctional facilities are "financially damned if they conform to the institutional environment, and ideologically damned -- socially, legally, and politically -- if they do not conform" (p. 586).

The private sector must attempt to maintain positive conditions of confinement as a means of retaining legitimacy within the institutional environment schema. Opponents of privatization, focusing on the institutional environment, have suggested conditions of confinement among other features of the private correctional facilities (e.g., employee salary and benefits) will suffer at the hands of the technical environment. If private correctional facilities focus on legitimacy problems such as maintaining conditions of confinement, they would face increasing costs (Ogle, 1999). Proponents of privatization don't question the legitimacy of private corporations [with exceptions of concerns of accountability (see Harding, 1997)] but instead have a focus on the technical environment. They have suggested private correctional facilities hold promise in areas of economic efficiency in which the public sector has failed miserably by comparison.

The question left for exploration based on the organizational argument is whether the legitimacy of private correctional facilities is at stake given the nature of the technical environment in its profit seeking nature. If private facilities can demonstrate that a positive institutional environment exists through demonstrating high quality conditions of confinement, they would gain institutional legitimacy and examinations of the technical environment would be necessary. If a negative institutional environment is found to exist, institutional legitimacy would be lost and in turn challenge the technical environment. This could lead to a loss of public (and governmental) support.

Economic. Economic arguments surrounding privatization have focused on the cost-effectiveness of private facilities compared to public facilities. It has only been in the last decade that researchers have undertaken empirical research on the issue. Scholars examining cost effectiveness have debated the position that private corporations can provide correctional services at a lower cost than governmental agencies (Pratt & Maahs, 1999).

Additionally, scholars have discussed the difficulties associated with developing an accurate assessment of the cost effectiveness of private facilities in comparison to public facilities (Ryan, 1993). McDonald (1990) speculated that it may be due to these difficulties that researchers have delayed the investigation of the cost effectiveness issue. McDonald suggested that "developing an accurate assessment requires having more complete and comparable cost data than are easily available, and differences in accounting principles used by the private and public sectors must be recognized and overcome" (p. 395).

Proponents of privatization have provided a variety of reasons that private correctional facilities might enjoy greater cost savings as compared to public facilities (McDonald, 1990). They have argued that the private facilities can be more productive in procurement decisions and labor relations because they are able to avoid the "red tape" which the public sector must work through. Privatization allows for simplified hiring practices, labor allocation and the implementation of disciplinary actions since the employees of private facilities do not generally have an organized union. Additionally, since the private sector is profit seeking, they are thereby motivated to utilize available resources more efficiently. In contrast to the public sector, companies may provide employees in the private correctional facilities with incentives to discover and implement ways of increasing productivity, thereby increasing their profit margin.

Opponents of privatization have directly criticized each of the above claims. Simplified hiring practices and non-unionized workers may lead to the hiring of inept, unskilled and inexperienced correctional staff. These types of workers could contribute to poor conditions of confinement and would lead to an increased propensity toward abuse of their power position. In responding to the claim of incentives toward efficiency, opponents have suggested that while "the stimulus of seeking profits may have its advantages, the incentive to minimize costs may also encourage reductions in service quality" (McDonald, 1990, p. 397). The reduction in service quality that is of greatest concern is the overall deterioration in the conditions of confinement in the correctional environment leading to an unsafe and non-therapeutic environment.

Pratt and Maahs (1999) have summarized the claim of cost effectiveness within the private sector as inconclusive in reviewing the majority of the empirical evidence. Some empirical studies have claimed that private correctional facilities are more efficient than their public sector counterparts while other studies have reached the exact opposite conclusion (Winn, 1996). Other researchers have suggested they have not proven the cost savings of private correctional facilities (U.S. G.A.O., 1991), and when some research does demonstrate cost savings, the savings may actually be due to "low balling" of estimated costs. Thus, the companies may realize profits through utilizing fewer correctional officers who are inexperienced (Shichor & Sechrest, 1995). Additionally, studies have not included factors such as the variations in the economy of scale of the correctional facility (i.e., its ability to get bulk rate services because of large numbers of offenders), the age of the facility, and the security level variations in the "effectiveness equation" (Logan, 1990; Shichor & Sechrest, 1995).

The recent study by Pratt and Maahs (1999) provided evidence that holds promising answers to the cost-effectiveness question. They completed a meta-analytic study that reviewed 33 cost-effectiveness evaluations from 24 independent studies. They concluded that private correctional facilities were no more cost effective than public correctional facilities and other facility characteristics such as the facility's economy of scale, age and security level were the strongest predictors of the offender's per diem costs in the facilities.

Even if supporters and opponents ever agree upon an answer to the question of cost-effectiveness of private facilities, a number of related issues will remain. Related to cost effectiveness is the manner of cost cutting by profit seeking private companies to attain profits and its impact on the environmental quality of the correctional facilities.

Environmental Quality. Another way to examine the impact of privatization on offenders is through considering the quality of the correctional facility environment. Researchers examining the issue of environmental quality have addressed a variety of issues including the conditions of confinement in the correctional facilities, differences in the correctional population served, and the qualifications of the staff in the private correctional facilities (Logan, 1992).

In his book, Private Prisons: Cons and Pros (1990), Charles Logan presented the debate on the effect of privatization on quality of conditions of confinement from both sides of the issue. As Logan suggested, the fundamental question that underlies the issue of the quality of private facilities is whether privatization increases the quality of imprisonment due to innovations by private companies or whether commercial companies cut corners to save costs and thereby lower the quality of the correctional facility environment.

Proponents of privatization have argued that private correctional facilities provide competition for public correctional facilities forcing both the public and private sector to raise the quality of conditions of confinement as well as to provide a comparison or measuring rod for public facilities. As Harding (1998) suggested "in the long run, the most robust justification for privatization may lie in its impact on the performance of the public sector with consequential improvement of the system as a whole" (p. 647). However, this new alternative to state run facilities threatens the job security of employees within public facilities. Consequently, unions of the correctional staff of these facilities continue to monitor the expansion of private facilities and maintain a steadfast opposition to their development.

Opponents of privatization have suggested that contracting out to private corporations could reduce the quality of conditions because of the pressure to cut corners due to the profit seeking nature of the private sector. Opponents often view the cost savings of privatization as "cost cutting" in order to increase their profit margin. It must be considered, however, that private corporations may attain a higher level of efficiency (thus, cost savings) because of the public sector's mismanagement and grossly inefficient use of the same funds. It may not be drastic corner cutting but simply more effective utilization of the same resources that leads to cost savings. Thus, we could expect that private correctional facilities maintain the quality of conditions of confinement. One aspect that either side cannot ignore is that contracting could hardly do worse than some current conditions in existing public correctional facilities (Logan, 1992).

Harding (1997) proposed that the key issue in privatization is whether "in remaining pay master but delegating service delivery, the state truly does retain control over standards" (p. 2). In exploring the issue of quality of conditions of confinement, researchers have used performance-based models such as Logan's Quality of Confinement Indices to measure the offender and staff perceptions of the correctional facility environment. In the next chapter I explore the use of performance-based models and present some of the common models that researchers have used to measure the correctional facility environment.

A second issue related to environmental quality of private correctional facilities is the composition or the "skimming" of the offender population. Logan (1992) defined skimming as "the possibility that private correctional facilities may be able to decide which cases they will accept, or that the government will place only the less problematic cases with a contractor, retaining the more difficult cases itself" (p.121). Some private companies, such as Eclectic Communications, have clauses within their contract which allows them to reject offenders whom they feel are likely to "cause them trouble" (Logan, 1990). Harding (1998) emphasized that skimming of the population would merely be indicative of the cautious nature of government authorities in proceeding with correctional facility privatization. In essence, a selection bias may occur within private facilities that not only makes them incomparable to public facilities but also opens the door to discriminatory practices. The question becomes what types of populations exist in private facilities and do they differ from the population left to the public sector?

One of the dangers in the skimming of the offender population is the potential for discrimination against offenders. If a specific racial or gender group becomes labeled as a "problem group," skimming may allow for racism and discrimination to influence the admission criteria, keeping some groups out of private facilities. This becomes a problem if private facilities provide more positive conditions of confinement, therapeutic programming or other advantages and they exclude some groups from this environment.

A limited number of studies have examined the differences in the demographic composition of public and private facilities. A 1985 census survey found significantly different populations existed in private versus public adult facilities. This survey found private correctional facilities held a higher percentage of non-delinquent offenders, fewer minority offenders (37% vs. 53% in public facilities) and more women, as compared to public facilities (Krisberg et al., 1986).

By contrast, Shichor and Bartollas (1990) reported limited demographic differences between delinquents placed into public and private facilities by a Southern California probation department. Further, their study found juveniles in private facilities more often had family, psychological and physical problems than those placed in public facilities. While juveniles in private facilities seemed to have a greater number of psychological problems, juveniles in public facilities had committed offenses at an earlier age, had more prior offenses, had more frequent probation revocations, and had significantly higher involvement in gang activities. It may be however, that juveniles were equally distressed but these differences were attributable to differences in detection. Advocates of private facilities frequently have argued that a higher level of professional and treatment services are available at private facilities (Bartollas, 1997; Shichor & Bartollas, 1990).

Through impacting the admissions criteria of a correctional facility, skimming may also impact the levels of adjustment experienced by offenders. The correctional literature has examined adjustment to the correctional facility environment from primarily two theoretical perspectives: Importation theory and Deprivation theory. Researchers have utilized these perspectives to examine a variety of pre-institutional and institutional related factors to determine correlates of offender adjustment to institutional life. Adjustment is most often determined through number of disciplinary violations incurred by an offender (Goetting & Howsen, 1986): a large number of disciplinary violations are indicative of failure to adjust to the correctional facility environment. More recently researchers have measured adjustment using psychological and attitudinal measures as reported by the offenders (Gover, Styve, & MacKenzie, 2000).

The importation perspective argues that the subcultures, which exist within correctional facilities, reflect similar subcultures that exist outside of the correctional facility. The offenders have often formed these external subcultures based on factors such as ethnic composition or other individual characteristics. These subcultures are found to typically have norms and values that compete within the general population (Irwin & Cressey, 1962). Similar to these external subcultures, the subcultures formed in correctional facilities compete with one another to have their norms and values be dominant and thus elicit the goal of control over the correctional facility environment (Jacobs, 1976; Stojkovic, 1984). This competition results in disciplinary violations within the correctional facility when an offender attempts to gain this control over their environment. Importation theory suggests that the individual factors used to form these subcultures will also impact offender adjustment. Thus, Importation theory focuses on the demographic characteristics and pre-institutional experiences of the individual that they "import" into the correctional facility and may impact assimilation within the correctional facility environment (Lawson, Segrin, & Ward, 1996).

Studies have demonstrated that multiple pre-institutional characteristics of offenders on which offenders form subcultures significantly impact institutional adjustment (Harrer & Steffensmeier, 1996; MacDonald, 1999; MacKenzie, 1987). Age has consistently been one of the strongest predictors of correctional facility adjustment (Goetting & Howsen, 1986; Jensen, 1977; Wolfgang, 1961). It has been measured in a variety of ways including current age, age at commitment, and age at latest sentencing. Studies relate all these variations of age to correctional facility misconduct generally indicating younger individuals have higher levels of misconduct in correctional facilities.

Individual level factors, other than age, have provided less conclusive evidence. For example, studies examining race have found conflicting results, in some studies the relationship between race and levels of misconduct was not significant (Wolfgang, 1961), other studies have found African Americans to have a higher rate of misconduct (Getting & Hassan, 1983) or conversely a lower rate of misconduct (Petersilia & Honing, 1980). Similarly, offenders with chronic drug and/or alcohol problems have demonstrated greater levels of disciplinary infractions (Flanagan, 1983), fewer disciplinary infractions (Myers & Levy, 1978) or as having no relationship with infractions (Jaman, Coburn, Goddard, & Mueller, 1966) depending on the study consulted. While there is disagreement on which imported factors are primarily responsible for correctional facility adjustment, researchers agree on the necessity of including pre-institutional factors in models that explore adjustment.

The contrasting perspective to importation theory is deprivation theory, which focuses on factors inside the correctional facility walls that impact offender adjustment. As Parisi (1982) notes, "Imprisonment, according to this view, inherently deprives the inmate of basic needs, resulting in tension and particular ways of adapting" (p. 9). Theorists argue that institutional deprivation produces "pains of imprisonment" including the loss of personal security, material possessions, personal autonomy, and heterosexual relations which in turn affects their adjustment (Sykes, 1958; Sykes & Messinger, 1960). Offenders respond to these pains with increased levels of stress or negative attitudes. Goodstein and Wright (1989) emphasize the importance of the correctional facility environment concluding that "[correctional facilities] posses unique and enduring characteristics that impinge upon and shape individual behavior." (p. 265).

Researchers from the deprivation perspective have examined correctional facility specific variables and their impact on the degree of sub cultural assimilation within the facilities. Empirical evidence has related a variety of structural characteristics of correctional facilities to offender behavioral outcomes and attitudes including physical features, style of housing (e.g., cells versus dormitories), the noise levels, temperature, access, visibility and architectural aesthetics. Further, researchers have also linked factors such as lack of privacy, lack of offender control over their immediate physical environment (e.g., lighting) to increased pathology including aggression (Farbstein & Wener, 1982). Researchers have extensively studied the overcrowding of correctional facilities, they negatively relate overcrowding to physiological adjustment, increased psychiatric commitment, increased antisocial behavior and decreased pro-social behavior (Jan, 1980; Paulus, McCain & Cox, 1978). Thus, in addition to pre-institutional factors, which impact offender adjustment, we can also expect institutional factors to affect offender adjustment.

The most promising model incorporates tenants from both importation and deprivation theory since neither perspective clearly and completely predicts offender adjustment. Researchers have postulated and recently research has empirically supported the importance of the combined effect of the individual offender characteristics and the correctional facility environment as the most powerful determinant of adjustment (Bonta & Gendreau, 1988; Gover, Styve & MacKenzie, 2000; Porporino & Zamble, 1984; Wright, 1991).

A combined model of importation and deprivation factors is useful in exploring the impact of the operating sector in facilities on offender experiences and adjustment. If skimming does exist within private facilities, it could affect the admissions into the facilities and thus the pre institutional characteristics of the offenders. Following the importation and deprivation literature, we could expect that differences in offender populations in combination with the potential for differences in the institutional characteristics of the correctional facility environment could result in consistent differences in adjustment of offenders between private and public facilities.

This study will account for demographic characteristics of the offenders, their pre-institutional experiences and the institutional characteristics of the correctional facility environment to determine if differences exist between operating sectors in adjustment of the juvenile delinquents. The ideal adjustment measure would be misconduct and/or disciplinary violations to allow for comparison with the results from previous studies, however, these measures were only available for 68% of the facilities. Additionally, the available data varied greatly in its reliability. Alternatively, I will examine adjustment through self-reported psychological adjustment including levels of anxiety, depression, social bonds and pro-social attitude changes over time.

The last area that may be impacted by privatization of correctional facilities is the staffing of the facilities. Do private facilities attain profits through facilities employing fewer, less skilled staff to whom they offer minimal benefits and wages? One of the areas that are somewhat pliable to cost cutting is the number of staff members per shift and the pay and benefits offered to these staff (Austin, 1998). Because the salaries and benefits of positions within the private sector are generally less bountiful than the public sector it may be that new, inexperienced and poorly trained correctional staff are employed by the private correctional facilities. What effects would these differences in staff have on the quality of the correctional facility? Are the juvenile residents at greater risk of danger within the private facilities due to the lack of experience of the correctional officers? Are the correctional officers more likely to respond to situations with inappropriate use of force due to their lack of experience?

Conversely, there may be advantages in hiring new staff from outside the correctional field (Hatry, Brounstein & Levinson, 1993). The lack of experience with the correctional system may result in the officers breathing new life into facilities with their higher levels of enthusiasm. They may be more innovative and fluid in their thinking when new situations or security issues arise. Finally, the background of staff employed by the private facilities may differ from the backgrounds of staff that public facilities employ in educational rather than experiential realms. Will this type of background provide the foundation for a higher quality correctional facility?

Conclusion. In summary, a variety of issues surround the debate on the privatization of correctional facilities. These debates range from differing philosophies on punishment to organizational and economic perspectives. It is my position that these perspectives have something in common, they all either directly or indirectly impact the experiences of individuals who live or work in private and public correctional facilities and thus impact the environmental quality. Consequently, I will empirically examine these two environments to determine if significant differences in the environmental quality of conditions of confinement between publicly and privately operated juvenile correctional facilities exist. Further, I will also examine the impact of privatization on the adjustment of juvenile delinquents held in these correctional facilities and the experiences of staff that these correctional facilities employ.

CHAPTER 3

Conditions of Confinement in Juvenile Correctional Facilities

Quality management has been a driving force in recent years in the redesign of private organizations and corporations; only recently have scholars applied these concepts to public agencies (Jablonski, 1991). Osborne and Gaebler's book, Reinventing Government (1992), was key in describing how we could develop performance-based standards for public agencies. In 1993, Congress passed the Government Performance and Results Act (GPRA) with the purpose of improving "the efficiency and effectiveness of Federal programs by establishing a system to set goals for program performance and to measure results." The law attempts to improve program management through the process of operationalizing strategic plans, and specifying outcome measures and how researchers will evaluate them. Program managers can then make budget allocations with the help of this performance information.

While the use of such performance standards in public agencies is relatively new, it has important implications for use in correctional agencies (MacKenzie, Styve & Gover, 1998). Rather than depending upon reports of the success of some program, such performance standards would require clear evidence of program impact. There are several lines of research that have begun to move in the direction of quality management for corrections (e.g., Logan's quality of confinement indices, OJJDP's Conditions of Confinement Study, BJS/Princeton project reviewing papers on performance-based standards for justice agencies). These projects are attempts to quantify the aspects of the environment that researchers can use as indices of the quality of the environment. Frequently measures of success in corrections (e.g., recidivism) are dependent upon numerous factors (number of police officers, drug availability, social decay) that are not directly under the control of correctional administrators. Recognizing this, several criminologists have advocated that we can evaluate correctional programs based on intermediate outcomes as well as long-term outcomes.

Two other lines of work have sparked discussions within the criminal justice community about the need to measure the conditions or components of the environment. These works are: (1) rethinking performance measures for criminal justice, and (2) performance-based standards for corrections. Performance measures have been the topic of a recent Bureau of Justice Statistics-Princeton Project (DiIulio, 1993). The working group proposed that we should rethink the use of traditional criminal justice performance measures. In particular, DiIulio (1993) argues that while rates of crime and recidivism may represent basic goals of public safety, they are not the only, or necessarily the best, measures of what criminal justice facilities do. He advises criminal justice agencies to develop mission statements that include any activities that we can reasonably and realistically expect the agency to fulfill (DiIulio, 1991). In line with this is Logan's (1992) emphasis on evaluating correctional facilities on the day-to-day operations, not on ultimate, utilitarian goals of rehabilitation or crime reduction. Likewise, Petersilia (1993) argues that along with their public safety functions, we should evaluate community corrections on other activities such as the accuracy, completeness, and timeliness of pre-sentence investigations, monitoring of court-ordered sanctions, and how well they do in assisting offenders to change in positive ways. Thus, not only are these researchers emphasizing the need to investigate components or conditions of the environments that they study but also the need to use a wider range of measures to examine effectiveness.

The second focus of much attention in the corrections community has been on the standards used for corrections. Traditionally, these standards have been based on the opinions of experts in the field. However, recently, there has been a push toward verifying the validity of these standards through the use of data on actual performance (performance-based standards). High rates of conformance with nationally recognized standards, such as American Correctional Association Accreditation, do not necessarily mean that all is well. Many of the existing standards specify procedures and processes that programs should follow, but not the outcomes that they should achieve (U.S. D.O.J., O.J.J.D.P., 1994). These performance-based standards tie the standards to the desired performance or outcomes desired.

Three examples of the more common performance-based models that are appropriate for measuring the environments of the juvenile correctional facilities are: Quality of Confinement indices used by Logan (1990), OJJDP's Conditions of Confinement Study completed by Parent (OJJDP, 1994), and The Prison Environment Inventory (PEI) developed and tested by Wright (1985). In all of these models the researchers developed quantitative scales used to measure aspects of the correctional environment.

Logan's Quality of Confinement Model

Logan (1990) assumes a confinement model of imprisonment. According to Logan, the essential purpose of imprisonment is "to punish offenders-fairly and justly-through lengths of confinement [that are] proportionate to the seriousness of their crimes." This perspective ignores the mission of rehabilitation, deterrence and incapacitation. The confinement model argues that society has sent offenders to correctional facilities as punishment not for punishment. Coercive confinement carriers with it an obligation to meet the basic needs of offenders, a constitutional standard of fairness, due process as well as procedural justice with which we impose confinement. The mission statement of the confinement model of imprisonment as defined by Logan is "to keep prisoners - to keep them in, keep them safe, keep them in line, keep them healthy and keep them busy-and do it with fairness, without undue suffering and as efficiently as possible."

Logan also suggested that if we accept this model of confinement, it follows that we should shift our evaluation focus away from "hard to determine" outcomes to the observable processes within the correctional facility environment. He postulated eight dimensions for evaluating the quality of the correctional facility environment: Security, Safety, Order, Care, Activity, Justice, Conditions, and Management. Researchers have since implemented these indicators of the quality of the environment in a number of studies of the conditions of confinement in adult correctional facilities.

One of these studies, conducted in 1992, examined the differences in the quality of conditions of confinement between an adult public and an adult private correctional facility. Logan compared the environment of a state operated 200 bed, full-security correctional facility which housed female offenders in New Mexico with a new, privately operated facility and a federally operated correctional facility. The study assessed the correctional facility environments using offender and staff ratings of the environment as well as institutional records. Project staff interviewed the offenders and staff from the state operated public facility in the first part of 1989. Subsequently, the state transferred the entire population of the state operated facility to a new, private facility in midyear 1989. Six months after the transfer, project staff interviewed both staff and offenders again. Logan's evaluation compared the staff and inmate's perceptions of the quality of the conditions of confinement in the state operated facility prior to the transfer with the quality of conditions of confinement at the private facility after the transfer. Additionally, Logan compared each of these two correctional facility environments to the environment of a federally operated female facility determined *a priori* to be well-run and of high quality.

Results from the interviews with offenders and staff and examinations of the official institutional records were analyzed using Logan's Prison Quality Index (PQI). The index combined the indicators from offender ratings, staff ratings and institutional records. Pair-wise comparisons of the Prison Quality Index scores indicated that the private correctional facility outperformed both the state and federally operated facilities in terms of quality of conditions. The exceptions were the Care and Justice indices wherein the public and private correctional facilities were not significantly different. Thus, Logan concluded the private correctional facility in his sample provided higher quality of conditions of confinement than the public correctional facilities.

However, the results were not that straightforward when the data sources (offender ratings, staff ratings, and facility records) were considered independently. Logan noted the staff data and, to a lesser extent, the institutional records primarily supported the overall finding of a more favorable private correctional facility environment. The offender ratings, however, demonstrated the state correctional facility outperformed the private correctional facility and the federal correctional facility in all indices with the exception of the Activity dimension. In essence, we should view Logan's findings as mixed support for the quality of the private correctional facility environment since it was only when he combines data sources that participants rated the private correctional facility more positively than the public correctional facilities. If the data sources were considered independently, it was clear that the staff and offenders had very different perceptions of many of the indicators of the quality of confinement. This finding highlights the importance of considering multiple perspectives when evaluating the quality of the correctional facility environment.

In addition to the caveat of the different results when Logan combines the data sources, it is also important to note other drawbacks of this study. Since many of the participants of the study from the state level facility were the same participants from the private facility (at a later time period), they may have been experiencing a halo effect due to the transfer to new surroundings. Thus, the change of environment and relative "newness" of the private facility may have enhanced the offender's positive perceptions. The majority of the staff had worked in the public correctional facility for a significant amount of time prior to their ratings of the environment; thus, it is possible that earlier experiences in the public correctional facility reflected negatively on the perception of that environment. It may have been more ideal to include a method of controlling for the age of the facility, individual characteristics of the offender population and work experiences of the staff.

Office of Juvenile Justice and Delinquency Prevention (OJJDP) Conditions of Confinement Model

As the result of a 1988 directive from Congress, OJJDP attempted to determine the extent to which conditions of confinement in juvenile correctional facilities throughout the U.S. conformed to recognized professional standards. Consequently, OJJDP researchers assessed 46 criteria that reflected existing national professional standards (from the American Correctional Association, the National Commission on Correctional Health Care, the American Bar Association) in 12 areas that represented advisers' perceptions of confined juveniles' most important needs in four broad areas (basic needs, order and safety, programming, juveniles' rights). They examined the association between these conditions and factors such as escapes, suicides and injuries.

The OJJDP study utilized three sources of data: (1) the 1991 Children in Custody Census; (2) a mail survey created by OJJDP; and (3) two-day site visits to 95 randomly selected facilities out of the 984 facilities that participated. The study used site visits to interview facility administrators and staff members as well as five randomly selected juveniles at each site (for a total of 475 juveniles). Based on this wealth of data, OJJDP researchers found that problems existed in several areas of conditions of confinement, specifically living space, health care, security and control of suicidal behavior. They also concluded facilities that conformed to national standards did not necessarily result in improved conditions of confinement. Finally, the study found a distribution of the deficiencies in conditions of confinement across a number of facilities. There were a very limited number of facilities that had no deficiencies in the conditions of confinement according to OJJDP's model. More specifically, between 35 and 49% of facilities met the indicators of the Basic Needs criteria, 27 to 51% of the facilities met indicators of Order and Security criteria, 57 to 85% met of the various Programming criteria, and 25 and 76% of facilities conformed to the Juvenile Rights indicators.

This study was an informative first step in a large scale assessment of the conditions of confinement in juvenile correctional facilities. Despite good response rates and an attempt to develop an objective means to measure the environment, this study has some limitations. One limitation is that the study did not consider the individual juveniles in the facilities and relied on facility level data. The result is an inability to determine how conditions of confinement in the facilities affect the juveniles' experiences in the correctional facility. Thus, we don't know if the facilities are meeting therapeutic needs of their offenders.

Wright's Prison Environment Indices (PEI)

The Prison Environment Indices, developed by Kevin Wright, was based on one of the most well known scales used in the measurement of institutional climates, the Correctional Institution Environment Scale (CIES). Moos (1971, 1974, 1975) developed the CIES to provide "an assessment of the social milieu of an institution." However, he failed to present either theoretical or empirical indicators for the 90 item scale (Wright & Bourdouris, 1982). Further, psychometric analysis failed to support Moos' categorizations.

As a result of this criticism, Wright turned to the work of Hans Toch (1977) to provide guidance in developing correctional facility environment indices. Toch developed his indices based on interviews with more than 900 adult offenders. Content analysis of the data collected from the interviews led Toch to identify eight central environmental concerns held by the offenders: Privacy, Safety, Structure, Support, Emotional Feedback, Social Stimulation, Activity, and Freedom. Based on Toch's eight dimensions, Wright began the iterative process of developing the 42 item Prison Environment Inventory (PEI). The existence of the eight dimensions originally suggested by Toch was confirmed through factor analysis.

In contrast to Logan's Quality of Confinement index, which has been primarily used to make comparisons between correctional facility environments, Wright (1983) used the PEI to identify the quality of the correctional facility environments and the relationship of various dimensions to offender adjustment during incarceration. In one study, Wright randomly selected a total of 942 participants from 10 New York State correctional facilities. Data were collected through paper and pencil surveys administered to offenders as well as from official institutional records. The surveys gathered the offenders' perceptions of the environment using the PEI while institutional records provided information on behavioral outcomes such as disciplinary reports, offender altercations, and disruptive behaviors (offender self reports supplemented the institutional records).

Wright found four of the eight dimensions of the environment (Structure, Support, Freedom, and Privacy) were significant predictors of disruptive offender behaviors. However, the indices were only significant predictors of behaviors measured through institutional (official) records and did not predict self reported adjustment outcomes.

In summary, the three models used to measure the quality of conditions of confinement that were briefly presented aim to quantify the environment that exists inside the correctional facility walls. Researchers have implemented OJJDP's Conditions of Confinement model to examine quality of the environment as they related to meeting basic needs and rights of the incarcerated population. Studies have frequently utilized Logan's Quality of Confinement index to make comparisons between two or more correctional facility environments to determine existing levels of quality. Studies have also used Wright's Prison Environment Inventory, based on the earlier work of Moos and Toch, to measure the quality of the correctional facility environment and determine its relationship with levels of offender adjustment.

The aim of this study encompasses all of the above approaches as it (1) examines the level of quality of conditions of confinement for individual facilities; (2) compares the quality of conditions of confinement between two different types of facilities, private and public; and (3) determines the relationship of the quality of conditions of confinement with the adjustment of juvenile delinquents across time. Further, the environmental measures of this study incorporate the environmental dimensions considered by the above models in addition to other models such as Gendreau and Andrew's Correctional Program Evaluation Inventory (1994) that measures aspects of the correctional facility environments that are indicative of the quality of therapeutic programs.

Development of the Conditions of Confinement Indices

As discussed, we may appropriately adapt several different models for measuring the environments of juvenile correctional facilities: OJJDP's Conditions of Confinement Study by Parent (1994); Quality of Confinement indices (Logan, 1990); the Prison Environment Inventory (PEI) (Wright, 1985); the Correctional Facilities Environment Scale (Moos, 1974); and others such as the Correctional Program Evaluation Inventory (CPEI) (Gendreau & Andrews, 1994), and the Prison Social Climate Survey that is used by the Federal Bureau of Prisons (1993). Although these authors gave different names to the scales, a closer examination of the questions contained in these scales indicates many similarities exist among the dimensions used to measure the environment (see Table 1). For example, Logan's Activity scale includes measures of whether offenders usually have something to do to keep themselves busy: amount of work, industry and educational involvement. Moos' Involvement scale considers how active the residents are while in the program. Although Logan and Moos approach this dimension from a slightly different angle, both scales address the issue of "keeping them busy." After I examined the questions in all these scales, I proposed thirteen scales consistent with the concepts measured by these previous researchers.

I developed items for each of the thirteen conditions of confinement representing the following constructs: (1) Control, the security measures exerted over the resident's activities within the facility and security to keep the residents in the facility; (2) Resident Danger, the resident's risk of being injured by other residents; (3) Danger from Staff, the resident's risk of being injured by staff members; (4) Environmental Danger, the resident's risk of being injured as a result of being institutionalized; (5) Activity, the level and variety of activities available to delinquents; (6) Care, the quality of interactions between juveniles and between staff and juveniles; (7) Risks to Residents, the risks to the residents as a result of facility conditions; (8) Quality of Life, the general social environment including the juvenile's ability to maintain some degree of individuality; (9) Structure, the formality of daily routines and interactions with staff and other residents; (10) Justice, the appropriateness and constructiveness of punishments given to the residents; (11) Freedom, the provision of choice of activities and movement to residents; (12) Programs, the availability and utility of therapeutic opportunities; (13) Preparation for Release, activities with juveniles prior to release to ease in the transition back to society.

In conclusion, I have discussed the rationale, development and use of performance-based standards in corrections. Three major models were presented which quantify and measure the conditions of confinement in the correctional facilities. A contrast of these models demonstrated numerous similarities between the dimensions of the indices, which allowed for the theoretical presentation of an overarching model of conditions of confinement encompassing multiple aspects of all the scales.

CHAPTER 4

Methodology

This study addresses five research questions related to the environmental quality debate on the privatization of correctional facilities:

1. Do the juvenile populations in private and public facilities differ in their demographic composition and risk levels?
2. Are there differences in the demographics characteristics, education level, and prior work experiences of correctional staff employed in private and public facilities?
3. Are the conditions of confinement perceived to be more favorable in private or public facilities by the juveniles and staff?
4. Do privately operated correctional facilities differentially impact the adjustment of juveniles?
5. Do privately operated correctional facilities differentially impact the work experiences of the correctional staff?

The first question addresses the argument that differences may exist between the offender population held in public and private facilities. Some researchers have claimed that the private sector houses delinquents who are less serious, leaving the more difficult and more expensive to manage juvenile delinquents in the hands of the public sector. Consequently, the critics of privatization have questioned the utility of private correctional facilities if they are only focused on handling the less serious offender populations. Critics of privatization expect that less serious juvenile delinquents will comprise the population in private correctional facilities. Criminogenic features (e.g., young age at 1st arrest, a high number of commitments to facilities, etc.), psychological problems, and substance abuse problems (drug, alcohol or both) demonstrate the delinquent's level of seriousness. Supporters of privatization expect few differences to exist between the correctional populations in private and public facilities. In this study, I examine differences in these demographic characteristics and risk factors of juvenile delinquents between private and public facilities.

The second research question addresses the argument that differences exist in correctional staff populations between the private and the public sector. Opponents of privatization have argued that companies realize profits in the private sector primarily through the utilization of fewer, less skilled correctional staff that companies offer less pay and minimal benefits as compared to their public sector counterparts. These opponents expect staff in private facilities to be less educated and to have less or no previous work experience in a correctional environment.

In contrast, supporters of privatization expect no significant differences in the backgrounds of the two correctional staff populations. They argue that their employees are often drawn from the pool of public sector employees. Public sector employees may tire of the public sector and are drawn toward higher pay or better opportunities in the private sector. Supporters also argue that private facilities are better able to recruit and hire qualified employees because there is less "red tape" in the hiring process. To examine this issue, this study compares the demographic characteristics, education levels, and previous work experience of the correctional staff in public and private facilities.

In the third research question I address whether differences exist between public and private juvenile correctional facilities in the conditions of confinement from the perspective of the juveniles and the staff. Opponents of privatization have suggested that the quality of conditions of confinement is compromised due to the profit seeking nature of the private sector. Those who support privatization argue that the quality of conditions of confinement will not suffer at the hands of private corporations. They suggest that private corporations employ younger, less experienced staff who are more eager to work and do their work well in comparison to state workers who are secure in their jobs and unmotivated. Thus, supporters of privatization expect that the private facilities have more positive conditions of confinement (more controlled, safer, more structured, etc.) when compared to public facilities. To examine the relationship between the operating sector (public versus private) and the conditions of confinement, this study compares perceptions measured at the individual level (e.g., juvenile and staff perceptions) while controlling for characteristics of the facilities (e.g., capacity, facility age, the intensity of the admission process, the type of programs) and of the individuals (e.g., demographics, risk levels and backgrounds).

Given the potential for environmental differences, it follows that the operating sector (public operation vs. private operation) together with the conditions of confinement of the facilities may impact the adjustment of the juveniles as well as the work experiences of the correctional staff (see Figure 1). This concern is the basis for the fourth and fifth research question of this study.

I expect conditions of confinement to impact juvenile delinquent's adjustment and work experiences of the correctional staff. I compare the adjustment of juveniles in the two types of facilities to determine whether differences exist in the delinquents' initial psychological state as well as their adjustment over time as a result of the operating sector (private versus public) and the conditions of confinement. Given that opponents of privatization expect that the quality of the private correctional facilities is poorer (less safe, less therapeutic), I also expect a negative impact of privatization on the adjustment of juvenile delinquents during incarceration.

Further, I compare the work experiences of the correctional staff between the two types of facilities to determine the impact of the operating sector and conditions of confinement on stress, staff communication and job satisfaction. I expect a poorer work environment for the staff (more stress) employed in private facilities resulting in a lower level of job satisfaction.

The data utilized in this study were previously collected through a grant from the National Institute of Justice (grant # 96-SC-LX-0001). Investigators designed the previous project, *A National Evaluation of Juvenile Correctional Facilities*, to examine differences between boot camps and traditional facilities with a primary focus on the perceptions of the conditions of confinement by juvenile delinquents and correctional officers. Given that the focus during the data collection phase of the project was on differences between types of programs, researchers and participants were not aware that investigators were going to examine the impact of the operating sector (private vs. public) on the conditions of confinement.

Participants

Data were collected from three distinct sources. Two of the sources were juvenile delinquents and correctional staff who were administered paper and pencil surveys. The third data source was official record information obtained through interviews with facility administrators or superintendents.

Facility Selection. In 1996, researchers from the National Evaluation of Juvenile Correctional Facilities project contacted juvenile correctional agencies throughout the United States to identify all existing boot camps programs for juvenile offenders. They identified A total of 50 programs in

27 states for participation in the study. They eliminated four programs from the sample of potential participants either because the programs were nonresidential programs or were in the developmental stage and would not be open in time to participate in the research. They invited the remaining 46 boot camp programs to participate in the evaluation, 59% of eligible boot camp programs agreed to participate.

Once the boot camp sites were determined, investigators identified a comparison facility for each boot camp program and invited to participate in the study. The comparison facility was selected in consultation with the agency responsible for the boot camp facility and/or the facility administrators at the participating boot camps. The selection process identified the correctional facility in which a juvenile delinquent would most likely be placed if the boot camp program had not been available. All comparison facilities were located in the same state as the participating boot camp program. The comparison facilities consisted of juvenile detention centers, forestry camps, ranches, and training schools. All comparison facilities invited to participate in the study agreed to do so.

Juveniles. The sample of juveniles consisted of 4,121 juveniles surveyed in 48 correctional facilities (2,288 surveyed at Time 1 and 1,833 surveyed at Time 2). Of these 48 facilities, the private sector operated 16 of the facilities and the public sector operated 32 facilities.

Staff. The correctional staff sample consisted of 1,362 employees in 48 facilities. The staff survey was administered once, coinciding with the Time 1 administration of the juvenile survey.

Facilities. During the visits to the sites, researchers completed facility surveys with the facility administrators in one-on-one interview settings. This resulted in 48 facility surveys. Administrators were also contacted via the telephone subsequent to the site visit to collect any outstanding information or to clarify information previously collected. The facility survey included questions requiring reference to summary data from official records but not the files of individual juvenile delinquents.

Design and Procedure

Site Visits. The duration of the site visits conducted at each of the 48 juvenile correctional facilities varied from 1 to 2.5 days depending upon the size of the facility, scheduling of activities and number of juveniles surveyed. Project researchers initially met with the facility administrator or superintendent for a briefing of the survey procedure and to answer staff member questions.[2] While at the facility, researchers completed a census survey of all available juvenile delinquents[3], provided surveys for the staff members, conducted a video survey (and a walkthrough checklist), interviewed the administrator and collected summary data from official records. This research focuses on the information obtained from the juvenile delinquents, staff and facility surveys.

Administration of Juvenile Survey. Researchers completed a census survey of the juveniles in the facility whenever possible with all facilities surveyed twice. Recall that the data were originally collected for a project that had a focus of comparing boot camps to traditional facilities. Accordingly, they designed the Time 1 administration of the survey to include juveniles shortly after their entry into the boot camp program. At the same time, they also surveyed juveniles held in the appropriate comparison facility. They designed the second survey administration, referred to as Time 2, to include juveniles just prior to release from the

---

[2] They carefully adhered to human subject procedures as required by the facilities and the University of Maryland's Institutional Review Board.

[3] Occasionally, juvenile delinquents were not available due to court visits or medical visits at outside facilities.

boot camp. The investigators matched the time interval between survey administrations in comparison facilities to the time interval between administrations for the corresponding boot camp. This time interval ranged from three to eight months.

The timing of the Time 1 and Time 2 surveys provided two "snapshots" or cross sectional views of the facility at two different points in time, an average of four months apart. Additionally, it provided a small subset of the juveniles whom they surveyed twice thus providing a longitudinal view. Of the total number of juveniles whom investigators solicited for participation in the study, 93.5 percent completed the survey at Time 1.[4] At Time 2, this rate was somewhat lower at 78 percent. One reason for the lower completion rate at Time 2 may be due to the repetitive nature of the survey. Participants who had previously participated in the study were less inclined to fill out the same information a second time. The lower Time 2 completion rate resulted in a smaller number of pretest-post test participants than originally anticipated (n=530).

Two project researchers administered surveys in a classroom-type setting with groups of fifteen to twenty juveniles. Once they handed out individual survey materials to participants, they provided a presentation of videotaped instructions and survey questions on televisions within the classroom setting. This procedure ensured a uniform administration process and provided assistance to those juveniles with reading disabilities or lower reading levels. The videotape, about 45 minutes in length, began with a narration by researchers of the consent form and an explanation of the survey materials that they had distributed to the juveniles. On the balance of the videotape, the narrators read aloud the survey questions

---

[4] It is interesting to note that juveniles found the last 105 questions in the survey more interesting because the survey asked specific, concrete questions about their experiences in the correctional facility. Most likely, this greatly helped in the high completion rate.

and answer options while providing visual cues of the response sheet. Project researchers were present during the administration to answer questions about the survey and provided clarification, as needed on individual survey items. The average completion time of the juvenile survey was forty-five minutes.

Administration of Staff Survey. During the site visits, investigators gave staff surveys to facility administrators, which administrators were to distribute to staff members. They asked all direct contact staff members (who have contact with the juveniles on a regular basis) to complete a staff survey. Project researchers recommended the administrators disseminate the surveys to staff members during a staff meeting at which time the administrator would allow them to complete the survey[5]. The average time for staff survey completion was thirty minutes. The overall response rate obtained from staff was 66%[6].

Instruments

Juvenile Survey. The juvenile survey included 266 questions pertaining to demographic characteristics, prior criminal history, criminal attitudes and experiences in the facility (see Appendix A). Thirteen of the 266 questions were open-ended. The remaining questions were based on a five-point Likert scale as well as yes-no and true-false scale formats. The survey included 17 demographic questions, 17 risk

---

[5]Administrators didn't follow this recommendation in all facilities. Some facilities asked staff to fill the surveys out during their shift or on their own time at home.

[6] The lower response rate to the staff surveys as compared to the juvenile surveys may be attributable to a number of factors including a lack of enthusiasm of administrators distributing the surveys, failure to provide staff ample work time to complete the surveys, and staff member indifference toward their workplace environment.

factor scales, 8 psychological outcome scales and 13 conditions of confinement scales.

Staff Survey. The 216-item staff survey contained 23 scales and 11 demographic questions (see Appendix B). Thirteen of the scales concerned staff perceptions of the conditions of confinement in their facilities. Six scales address staff experiences in the work environment: Staff Communication, Personal Stress, Support of Staff, Planning, Job Satisfaction, and Attitudes toward Residents. Additionally, the survey contained three sections concerning formal Grievances, perceptions of Treatment Effectiveness, and Perceived Institutional Goals.

Facility Survey. The facility survey consisted of 244 questions, which required an average of two hours to complete. The facility survey provided information on key topics collected from facility records such as incident logs, disciplinary logs, grievance logs, and health care logs. Other information collected pertained to the facility's population, program components, capacity information, and personnel information. These data were collected for a one-year time period that dated back from the initial interview date. The facility survey did not require a review of individual juvenile records.

CHAPTER 5

Scale Analyses

This chapter begins with a brief description of the various scales that I use in this study. I have categorized these scales as juvenile risk, juvenile adjustment, staff work experiences, conditions of confinement and facility descriptors. I used Cronbach's alpha (1951) to assess the internal consistency of the items incorporated into each rationally developed scale. I formed the scales based on the sum of the individual item's scores, reversing the scoring for statements that negatively correlated with the underlying construct. All item responses within each scale had the same response options thus standardization of the scores was unnecessary. I computed scale scores for each participant by summing the individual scores of the items then dividing by the number of questions answered in that scale[7,8].

---

[7]If an individual failed to respond to more than 75% of the items in the scale, I did not compute a score. Overall, less than 10 % of the data were missing for conditions of confinement scales.

[8]Factor analysis with Varimax rotation was also completed to verify the items factor analyzed into a one-factor solution or each scale (Comrey & Lee, 1992). I compared scale scores to factor scores obtained from factor analysis of the scale items with Varimax rotation. All scales were found to correlate .96 or higher with the resulting factor scores.

Juvenile Risk Scales

The scales that I included in the juvenile survey measured three characteristics of juvenile risk levels as indicated by: (1) Alcohol Abuse, frequency and extent of alcohol consumption as well as lifestyle difficulties experienced as a result of alcohol use (α = .70), (2) Drug Abuse, frequency and extent of drug use as well as lifestyle difficulties experienced as a result of drug use (α = .54), and (3) Family Violence and Child Abuse, the extent to which a juvenile was either the witness or victim of physical and/or sexual abuse within their family environment (α = .85).

Juvenile Adjustment Scales

I designated five scales to measure the juveniles' reactions to the environment and the changes they experienced while in the facility (see Appendix A for detailed descriptive information and individual items): (1) Dysfunctional Impulsivity (Dickman, 1990), a tendency to act before thinking of consequences (α = .66), (2) Pro-Social Attitudes (Jessness, 1962), level of normative opinions with respect to authority figures and antisocial acts (α = .78), (3) Depression, indications of state level depression (α = .76), (4) Anxiety (α = .71), indications of state level anxiety (Spielberger et al., 1970), and (5) Social Bonds including ties to family, ties to school, ties to work (α = 84).

Staff Work Experience Scales

Information obtained from the staff self-report surveys allowed for the comparison of the experiences of the staff in the private facilities versus the staff in the public facilities. This study compares the prior experiences of the staff including (1) stress levels (α = .93), (2) level of job satisfaction ($\alpha = .89$), (3) support of staff ($\alpha = .88$), and (4) level of staff communication ($\alpha = .93$) (See Appendix B for scale items).

Conditions of Confinement Scales

I rationally developed thirteen conditions of confinement scales on the basis of earlier work as discussed in chapter three (Logan, 1990; Moos, 1974; OJJDP, 1994; U.S. Federal Bureau of Prisons, 1993; Wright, 1983). Items previously utilized in measuring the correctional facility environment were incorporated in addition to newly developed items (see Mitchell, MacKenzie, Styve & Gover, 1999 and Styve, MacKenzie, Gover, & Mitchell, 2000 for scale development rationale). The goal of the scale construction was to reduce the large number of questions measuring the environment into a smaller number of dimensions for use in the subsequent analysis.

I developed items for thirteen conditions of confinement scales with scores ranging from 1 to 5. Higher scores indicated a higher level of that condition. The scales developed were: (1) Control, the security measures exerted over the resident's activities within the facility and security to keep the residents in the facility ($\alpha = .70$); (2) Resident Danger, the resident's risk of being injured by other residents ($\alpha = .81$); (3) Danger from Staff, the resident's risk of being injured by staff members ($\alpha = .83$); (4) Environmental Danger, the resident's risk of being injured as a result of being institutionalized ($\alpha = .73$); (5) Activity, the level and variety of activities available to delinquents ($\alpha = .79$); (6) Care, the quality of interactions between juveniles as well as between the staff and the juvenile delinquents ($\alpha = .73$); (7) Risks to Residents, the risks to the residents as a result of facility conditions ($\alpha = .76$); (8) Quality of Life, the general social environment including residents' ability to maintain a reasonable degree of individuality ($\alpha = .67$); (9) Structure, the formality of daily routines and interactions with staff and other residents ($\alpha = .72$);

(10) Justice, the appropriateness and constructiveness of punishments given to the residents ($\alpha = .77$); (11) Freedom, the provision of choice of activities and movement to residents ($\alpha = .64$); (12) Programs, the availability and utility of therapeutic opportunities ($\alpha = .90$); (13) Preparation for Release, activities with juveniles prior to release to ease in the transition back to society ($\alpha = .45$) (see Appendix A).

Facility Descriptors

I developed two indices from data collected in the facility survey to aid in the descriptions of the populations housed within these facilities (see Appendix C). The Admission Process Index contained items that indicated the intensity of the admission process of the facility. The Population Seriousness Index included items pertaining to the criminal backgrounds of the juveniles to whom facilities would allow admission.

Analytical Models

This chapter concludes with a detailed outline of the analytical strategies I use to answer the research questions contained in this study. I have divided the analytical strategy into the following sections: Descriptors, Perceptions of Conditions of Confinement, and Impact of the Operating Sector on Juveniles and Staff.

Descriptors. Demographic characteristics and risk factor data collected in the juvenile, staff and facility surveys allow for a comparison of the population composition and other characteristics between the private and public juvenile correctional facilities. I examine a number of characteristics within the juvenile delinquent sample including gender, race, offense type, age, sentence length, time in the facility, alcohol abuse, drug abuse, family violence and child abuse, age at first arrest, and number of previous commitments to correctional facilities. Within the correctional staff sample, I will include in the model the characteristics of age, race, gender, education level, number of years employed at current correctional facility, and the number of years previously employed within other correctional facilities. The facility survey allows for the consideration of the types and regional location of programs, whether follow up information is collected on the juvenile delinquents (e.g., recidivism, return to school etc.), the maximum capacity of the facility, the age of the facility, the admission's process, the criminal seriousness of the population, the juvenile delinquent to staff ratios and the number of hours per week assigned for visitations.

To determine if the composition of the juvenile delinquent and correctional staff populations are significantly different between the two types of facilities (public and private operating sectors), I utilize a nested analysis-of-variance (ANOVA) model (Ott, 1988; Maxwell & Delany, 1989) for continuous variables and a random effects probit model for dichotomous variables. I have also utilized these same models to examine the differences between facility characteristics. The nested ANOVA model with mixed-effects considers the primary variable of interest, the operating sector, to be a fixed factor whereas the facilities (and individuals within them) are considered to be random effects. The operating sector is fixed because the nature of this study predetermines the levels of the operating sector to be either private or public. The effect of the facilities is considered to be random because they are drawn from the entire population of juvenile correctional facilities and is a reasonable representation of juvenile delinquents across all United States correctional facilities. Further, inferences made about the facilities in this sample under this modeling schema with the random effects are then generalizable beyond the sample to the population of correctional facilities across in the United States.

As stated above, this model includes error terms for both the random effects of individuals grouped by facilities as well as the error terms for the fixed effect of the operating sector of the facility with individual nested within facilities. The latter error term for the effect includes variability across facilities within operating sector and variability across individuals within facilities. The result is a more conservative estimate of the significance of differences between individuals in comparison with the *t* statistic. The primary statistic of interest in the nested ANOVA model is the main effect of the operating sector on the demographic indicators. The following model represents this nested design:

$$Y_{ijk} = \mu + \alpha\text{; with the error for } \alpha \text{ as } \beta_{kj} + \varepsilon_{ijk}$$

where *j* designates the fixed effect factor of the operating sector (private or public), *k* designates the facilities nested within the operating sectors and *i* designates juveniles within the *jk*th cell. To test the effect of the nested factor (individual scores within facilities), the model imposes restrictions to determine whether means within the factor of the operating sector are equal.

To determine whether the population compositions of juvenile delinquents and correctional staff are significantly different between the public and private facilities on characteristics of a dichotomous nature (i.e., gender, race, etc.), a random effect probit model is most appropriate. The probit model examines the impact of the operating sector on the dichotomous characteristic, accounting for the variability across facilities due to the operating sector and the variability across individuals within facilities (Conway, 1990).

Perceptions of Conditions of Confinement. I address a number of questions by examining the indices of quality of conditions of confinement using hierarchical linear modeling (HLM). This model makes a comparison between the 16 private and 32 public facilities, testing the main effect of the operating sector on the perceived conditions of confinement (dependent variable) controlling for a number of covariates. I utilize these models to test for significant differences between public and private facilities using both the perceptions of the juvenile delinquents and the correctional staff.

The hierarchical linear model is appropriate given the multiple levels of the data available. In comparing the perceptions of the juvenile delinquents, I have included individual level covariates such as age, gender, race, sentence length, length of time spent in the facility, age at first arrest, number of prior commitments, history of family violence, level of alcohol abuse, level of drug abuse, and offense type in the first level of the hierarchical model. In the models comparing the perceptions of the staff, I will include the first level includes covariates for age, gender, race, education level, years of prior correctional experience, and current length of employment at the facility.

The second level of the hierarchical linear model testing both juvenile and staff perceptions includes facility level data such as the operating sector (public or private), the type of program (boot camp, detention center or other), the population size of the facility (maximum capacity), the age of the facility, the juvenile to staff ratios, the number of hours scheduled per week for visitation, the intensity of the facility's admission process, the seriousness of the offender population and the region of United States in which the facility is located. I centered the predictors in the model around their grand mean where appropriate to allow for comparisons of individual perceptions across all facilities opposed to group mean centered which would only allow for comparisons of the individual perceptions to their individual facility mean.

I have constructed separate models for each of the thirteen conditions of confinement for the two sets of perceptions, juveniles and staff. The end product was twenty-six models that allowed for comparisons of the quality of conditions of confinement between private and public correctional facilities.

Impact of the Operating Sector on Juvenile Delinquent and Staff Experiences. Beyond the perceptions of conditions of confinement, I have examined the impact of the operating sector on the adjustment of the juvenile delinquents and the work experiences of the staff using the HLM modeling strategy. Both characteristics of the facility and characteristics of the individual could moderate the experiences of the juvenile delinquents and staff in the facilities (see Figure 1). In these models, the environmental conditions of confinement were aggregated to the facility level. The aggregated conditions of confinement variable and the characteristics of the individuals are used to predict juvenile adjustment in the time between the two survey administrations. In separate models, the aggregate conditions of confinement variable and the characteristics of the staff are used to predict the work experiences of the staff.

I measured the juveniles' adjustment through change in their self-reported levels of pro-social attitudes, anxiety, depression, dysfunctional impulsivity and social bonds between the Time 1 and Time 2 survey administration. The repeated measures of these scales determine whether the operating sector and the quality of the conditions of confinement impacts juvenile delinquent adjustment over time and whether characteristics of the population and facility mitigate the effects, as I have illustrated in Figure 1.

The effect of the operating sector and the quality of the conditions of confinement on work experiences of staff within the correctional facilities were examined using measures of stress levels, job satisfaction, support of staff and staff communication. Although the impact of the operating sector on juvenile adjustment is examined through change in outcome levels between Time 1 and Time 2, the impact of the operating sector on staff experiences is examined using only Time 1 because researchers had only administered the surveys to the staff once.

CHANPTER 6

Results

Juvenile Characteristics

I have outlined results of the juvenile demographic characteristics and risk level comparisons between private and public correctional facilities in Table 2. As indicated on the table, private facilities held a significantly higher percentage of males and a significantly higher percentage of juvenile delinquents incarcerated for property offenses as compared to the juvenile delinquents held in public correctional facilities. Other demographic comparisons were not statistically significant.

While there were limited differences between the private and public facilities on these juvenile delinquents' demographic and risk characteristics, I expect that these factors may impact individual perceptions of the quality of the conditions of confinement and the juvenile delinquent's adjustment over time. Therefore, I have included these variables as covariates in subsequent analyses.

These demographic comparisons address the first question of this study: Do the juvenile populations in private and public facilities differ in their demographic composition and risk levels? Despite concerns that skimming of the juvenile delinquents may result in dramatically different populations that are held in private and public correctional facilities, comparisons suggest that the two populations are not significantly different on the majority of the demographic and risk indicators with the exceptions of gender and offense. In particular, there is no evidence that private facilities are able to select delinquents who are at a lower risk for future criminal activities (e.g., low levels of substance abuse, older at first arrest).

Staff Characteristics

I have outlined the results from the demographic comparisons of the correctional staff characteristics between private and public facilities in Table 3. Using nested analysis of variance models and random effects probit models, statistically significant differences between correctional staff in private and public facilities were found in the mean age of correctional staff, the length of previous employment experience in correctional facilities and the current length of employment at the facility.

These findings address the second question of this study: Are there differences in the demographics characteristics, education level, and prior work experiences of correctional staff employed in private and public facilities? Private facilities were found to employ younger correctional staff who had less prior experience at correctional facilities. The private facilities had employed their staff for a significantly shorter period of time as compared to the correctional staff employed by public facilities. This shorter period of current employment and inexperience of the staff members at the private facilities could be attributed to the relative newness or expansion of private facilities. No differences were found in either the gender or racial distributions of the correctional staff. Further, there were no differences in the level of education of the staff between private and public facilities.

Facility Characteristics

In addition to comparing the juvenile delinquent and staff population compositions between private and public facilities, the data collected through interviews with the facility administrators allowed for comparisons between the characteristics of the facilities. These data were collected from the facilities' policy manuals, records, schedules or the common knowledge of the facilities' administrators.

As demonstrated in Table 4, I examined a variety of facility descriptors. Statistically significant differences were found between private and public facilities in their population capacity, facility age, and admission procedures. No significant differences were found in the criminal seriousness of the juvenile delinquents, the juvenile delinquent to staff ratios, or the number of hours scheduled by facilities for visiting.

As a proxy for the physical size, the maximum capacity for which contractors designed the facility demonstrates that private facilities are significantly smaller than public facilities. On average, private facilities hold less than half of the number of juvenile delinquents (M = 60 juveniles) than typically held in public facilities (M = 137 juveniles). Further, the physical structure of private facilities was found to be significantly newer (M = 4.4 years) than public facilities (M = 29.6 years).[9]

A series of questions posed to facility administrators formed the basis of the Admission Process Index (see Appendix C). This index ranges from 0 to 1 with higher scores indicating more intensive admission processes with greater input from the facility and more extensive evaluation of the delinquents prior to admission. The nested analysis of variance model indicates private facilities have a more

---

[9]The age of facility variable was not an indication of the age of the program but of the physical structure itself.

stringent admission process for juvenile delinquents who enter into their facilities. More specifically, a greater percentage of the private facilities had procedures in place that allowed personnel at the facility to interview and evaluate juveniles prior to admission on medical, physical and psychological criteria as compared to staff at public facilities. These more extensive evaluations may provide private facilities with the opportunity to disallow a juvenile admission into their facility for failure to meet specified program criteria (e.g., juveniles with a history of violence), a luxury that is not often afforded to public facilities.

In summary, these comparisons of facility characteristics between private and public juvenile correctional facilities indicate some important distinctions between the two types of facilities. Private facilities were significantly smaller programs housed in newer physical structures. Private programs had significantly more intensive admission processes which allowed for a more extensive evaluation of the juvenile delinquents that were sent to their facility. The more intensive admission protocol, however, did not lead to significant differences in the level of criminal seriousness of the population housed in the private facilities. Since the characteristics of the facilities examined herein could impact the conditions of confinement as perceived by the juveniles and staff, I include them as covariates in further examination of the perceptions of the conditions of confinement.

Juvenile Perceptions of the Conditions of Confinement

The first step in determining whether differences existed between private and public facilities in the juveniles' perceptions of conditions of confinement examined the means of each of the thirteen conditions. I implemented nested analysis of variance models to initially test for statistical significance, unadjusted for covariates.

Table 5 contains the means for private and public facilities for each of the thirteen conditions of confinement listed in Column 1. All scale scores range from a low of one to a high of five. A higher score on the scale indicates a higher level of the condition. For example, a control scale score of 3.2 indicates a higher level of facility control when compared to a control scale score of 2.5. The more ideal correctional environment would have higher scores on the first eight environmental conditions (i.e., control, activity, care, quality of life, justice, therapeutic programming, and preparation for release) and low scores on the next five environmental conditions (i.e., resident danger, danger from staff, environmental danger, risks to residents and freedom).

Mean differences between public and private facilities were tested for statistical significance using the nested analysis-of-variance framework. Recall, that this model includes error terms for both the random effects of individuals grouped by facilities as well as the error terms for the fixed effect of the operating sector of the facility with individual nested within facilities. And, the latter error term for the effect includes variability across facilities within operating sector and variability across individuals within facilities. The result is a more conservative estimate of the significance of differences between individuals in comparison with the t statistic. When I implement this framework, there are no statistically significant differences between the means of private and public facilities using the .05 criteria.

Most investigations of environmental differences between facilities have not continued with further empirical examination of their findings beyond these types of simple descriptive statistics. However, given that some statistically significant differences were found to exist between private and public facilities in both the composition of the juveniles' demographics and risk levels as well as the characteristics of the facilities, this issue needs further exploration. These differences must be considered to ensure that I have established a true picture of the conditions of confinement in these facilities. Thus, I need to apply a more complex model such as the hierarchical linear model (HLM). This model accounts for the influence of individual characteristics as well as the characteristics of the facilities. It is only with these results that I can make more definitive conclusions about the conditions of confinement in facilities.

I analyzed the perceptions of the conditions of confinement from the viewpoint of the juvenile delinquents in a stepwise manner using the HLM procedure. The first step in the analysis was to determine the contribution of the individual level characteristics of the juveniles (demographics and risk factors) in the explanation of the variability between facility means for each of the thirteen conditions of confinement. As noted earlier, the individual characteristics included in the model were age, gender, race (white versus nonwhite), sentence length, time in facility, age at first arrest, number of previous commitments, level of previous family violence and child abuse experienced, level of alcohol abuse, level of drug abuse, and type of offense (dummy coded for property, person, drug and other). The initial models, which included only individual characteristics of the juvenile population, indicated that significant variation remained across the facility means for all thirteen conditions of confinement models beyond the variance explained by the individual characteristics of the juveniles. The statistical significance of the chi square statistic indicated the need for the inclusion of facility variables at level two such as the operating sector (private versus public).

The second step in the model is the addition of the effect of the operating sector on the conditions of confinement along with the individual covariates. Table 6 displays the resulting operating sector coefficients from these models. As demonstrated, the operating sector significantly impacted the juveniles' perceptions of the environment in only one of the thirteen conditions of confinement, Activity. Results show that juveniles perceived significantly higher levels of activity in private facilities as opposed to public facilities. This coefficient was significant at the .05 level, all other coefficients failed to meet an even less stringent criteria of .10. Thus, it must be considered that given the number of models implemented, the statistical significance of the Activity model may be due to random chance.

In summary, the results from this model show that there are no significant differences between private and public juvenile correctional facilities in their conditions of confinement, except for activity level. The statistical significance of the χ^2 statistic in all thirteen models suggests that a significant amount of variation in the means across facilities is unexplained by the current model. Thus, the present model is not a good fit to the data. This result, combined with the earlier finding of statistically significant differences between other facility characteristics, indicates that a more complex model at level two is warranted.

It follows that the next step in the process is to include facility level variables beyond the operating sector variable. The facility level variables that were incorporated into the model were the type of program (dummy coded for boot camp, detention center, and training school excluding the category of other facilities), the capacity of the facility, the age of the facility, the juvenile to staff ratios, the number of hours scheduled for visitations, the intensity of the admission process, the seriousness of the offender population and dummy variables for the region of the United States in which the facility is located. With the addition of the facility level variables to the individual level variables, the full model for testing the effect of the operating sector on perceived conditions of confinement was in place.

There is a limitation that I should note in using this full model. Only 48 facilities exist within the data set, which results in 48 degrees of freedom at level 2 of the hierarchical linear model. Once I include the numerous variables at the facility level, there are limited degrees of freedom remaining in the model. The result is low statistical power and the potential for over fitting the data. Thus, coefficients that may have an impact on the dependent variable might not demonstrate statistical significance.

I have displayed the results from the full model in two separate tables (Table 7 and Table 8) due to the numerous variables included and the multiple dependent variables. Table 7 includes the unstandardized beta coefficients for each of the facility level variables across the thirteen conditions of confinement. Since the dependent variables are of the same scale ranging from one to five, we are able to compare coefficients between each of the thirteen dependent variable models. I list the dependent variables in Column 1 and the independent variables across the top of the table in Row 1 to facilitate comparisons of coefficients. I have listed the primary variable of interest, the operating sector, in Column 2 of Table 7. I have coded this variable such that public facilities are equal to zero and private facilities are equal to one.

As indicated in Column 2 of Table 7, the absolute values of the coefficients displayed the effects of the operating sector on the juvenile's perceptions for each of the thirteen conditions of confinement range from .02 to .21. The unstandardized beta coefficients demonstrate statistical significance in only one condition of confinement, Structure (B = -.19). This coefficient indicates that juveniles in private facilities perceived significantly less structure in their environment than juveniles in public facilities, controlling for numerous facility and individual level characteristics. However, the statistically significance of Structure is likely due to random chance given the number of models that have been analyzed.

In summary, these models address the first part of the third question in this study: Are the conditions of confinement perceived to be more favorable in private or public facilities by the juveniles [and staff]? Once the models include covariates for the individual and facility characteristics, there are no statistically significant differences between public and private juvenile correctional facilities.

Facility Level Covariates. Beyond the public-private facility comparisons, these models provide insight into other factors which impact juveniles' perceptions of their conditions of confinement. Table 7 also outlines the beta coefficients for all other facility level variables included in the models for each of the thirteen conditions of confinement.

One of the variables that had a strong impact on the conditions of confinement was the indicator of whether "follow-up information" was available. This variable indicated whether the facility collected or if an agency provided the facility with follow-up information on the juveniles that left their correctional facility, which included the receipt of recidivism data, re enrollment in school and so forth. The variable is dichotomous with a designation of one, indicating follow-up information is collected or available to the facility and a zero if no such information is collected or available. The absolute values of the coefficients for "follow up info" ranged from .01 to .54.

Two other facility variables that exhibited a strong impact on the conditions of confinement were type of program and region. Results demonstrated that the perceptions of the conditions of confinement varied depending upon the type of program. Given the variety of program approaches including forestry programs, detention centers and boot camps, it is not surprising that juveniles perceived varying level of control, structure and so forth within these different program approaches. Regional differences were also found to exist. The regions were dummy-coded excluding the regional grouping of the Southern states; consequently, I compared all other regions to the South. The greatest differences in the conditions of confinement were found between the Southern and Eastern regions of the country. Specifically, the Eastern region was found to have more positive conditions of confinement than the Southern region.

Individual Level Covariates. In addition to providing insight into facility level characteristics that effect the juveniles' perceptions, these models also allow for the exploration of individual factors that significantly contribute to these perceptions. Table 8 displays the unstandardized beta coefficients for each individual characteristic (juvenile demographics and risk factors) across the thirteen conditions of confinement. Overall, the effects of these individual covariates on the perceptions of the conditions of confinement are only moderate. The absolute values of the coefficients range from .00 to .22 with strong effects demonstrated by age at first arrest, race and child abuse.

The age of the juvenile at the time of their first arrest was found to significantly impact nine of the thirteen conditions of confinement. Results demonstrated that the older the juvenile was at first arrest, the more positive they perceived the environment. Specifically, they reported the environment to have significantly higher levels of control, activity, care, structure, and justice as compared to juveniles first arrested at an older age. They also reported greater benefits from the therapeutic programs and felt more prepared for release back into the community. Further, juveniles first arrested at an older age perceived the environment to have significantly lower levels of environmental dangers and risks to residents.

The two other variables that demonstrate a statistically significant impact on the juveniles' perceptions of the conditions of confinement are race and the level of family violence and child abuse. I have coded race into White (1) and Nonwhite (0). The Nonwhite category encompasses African Americans, Hispanics, American Indians, Asians as well as individuals who indicated the categorization of "other." As the coefficients in Table 8 indicate, juveniles who were White perceived an environment that is more structured and just. Further, they felt the therapeutic programming was less beneficial and perceived a lower level of danger from staff and the environment as well as fewer risks to residents. The converse interpretation is that juveniles who were Nonwhite perceived a less structured and just environment that had more danger from staff and higher levels of risks to residents. However, Nonwhite juveniles did perceive the therapeutic programming to be more beneficial.

The finding of racial differences in the perceptions of conditions of confinement leads to important questions and concerns regarding equality of treatment in juvenile correctional facilities. Are the perceptions of higher levels of danger and lower levels of justice attributable to perceptual differences of the environment or unequal treatment? Although these data do not allow for an answer to this question, it is an important question that we should investigate in future research.

The second variable that demonstrates predictive ability is the level of family violence and child abuse. Recall that this scale is a five-point scale with higher scores indicating a more serious self reported history of abuse and/or viewing of violence within the individual's family. The models indicated statistical significance of the effect of family violence and child abuse history on all conditions of confinement except for freedom. As shown in Table 8, juveniles with a more serious abuse history perceived the environment to have lower levels of control, activity, care, quality of life, structure, and justice. They perceived less benefit from the therapeutic programming and felt less prepared for release into the community. Additionally, they perceived more danger from all sources as well as greater risks to residents.

As with the finding of differences in racial perceptions, these negative perceptions by juvenile delinquents with a history of abuse are cause for concern. These findings demonstrate that the criminal justice system is not meeting the needs of one of the most desperate populations. Individuals with histories of abuse do not feel safe in these correctional environments and they perceive the treatment that the programs offer to be less effective in general nor specifically in their transition back to the community.

<u>Conclusion.</u> In conclusion, the juvenile delinquents' perceptions of the conditions of confinement have indicated that there are no

significant differences between the conditions of confinement in public and private correctional facilities. These models have also provided important insight on factors impacting conditions of confinement through the exploration of covariates at both the facility and individual level in these models. Of specific concern is the finding that juveniles with histories of family violence and child abuse as well as juveniles who are minorities perceive the conditions of confinement in correctional facilities to be significantly more negative. The next step in exploring the conditions of confinement question is to confirm the above finding from the perspective of the correctional staff.

Staff Perceptions of the Conditions of Confinement

I examined the staff perceptions of the conditions of their work environment following the same protocol used to examine the juvenile perceptions. The first step in comparing the conditions of confinement between public and private facilities from the staff perspective was to examine the means. Table 9 displays the means for each of the thirteen conditions of confinement as perceived by the staff in both private and public facilities. Recall that these scales range from one to five with higher scores indicating a greater level of the dependent variable listed.

In examining the means, perceptions of staff are found to be amazingly similar to the perceptions of juveniles in the facilities. I tested the differences in means of the staff perceptions of the conditions of confinement between private and public facilities with the nested analysis-of-variance model. The results indicate that only two of the thirteen conditions of confinement indicate statistically significant differences between private and public facilities, Activity and Environmental Danger. As compared to public facilities, private facilities have significantly higher levels of activity and significantly lower levels of environmental danger from the perspective of the staff. However, given the large number of dependent variables, it is most likely that these differences are due to random chance.

The next step in the analysis of the staff perspective on the conditions of confinement was to control for the individual differences of the correctional staff members and the differences in the facility characteristics. I imposed a two-level hierarchical linear model on the perceptions of the staff. The first level of the model included individual characteristics of the staff including age, gender (male=1; female=0), race (white=1; nonwhite=0), education level, years of prior correctional experience, and length of employment at the facility. The second level of the model used the same variables as the models for the juveniles: the operating sector (public or private), type of program (boot camp, detention center or other), the population size of the facility (maximum capacity), the age of the facility, the juvenile to staff ratios, the number of hours scheduled for visitations, the intensity of the facility's admission process, the seriousness of the offender population and region of United States.

This hierarchical linear model analysis was completed in a stepwise manner. First, I used the individual level covariates of the staff to predict their perceptions of the conditions of confinement. The statistical significance of the χ^2 statistic in all thirteen models suggested that a significant amount of variation across the facility means that is unexplained by the current model. The present model is not a good fit to the data. This result, combined with the earlier finding of statistically significant differences between other facility characteristics, indicates that a more complex model is warranted. Thus, these results allow for the continued exploration of facility characteristics. Consequently, in the next step I included the effect of the operating sector on the staff perceptions of the conditions of confinement in addition to the individual covariates of the staff.

As shown in Table 10, the operating sector significantly impacted the staff perception of the conditions of confinement in five of the thirteen conditions. Staff perceived the environment of private facilities to have significantly higher levels of control and care, less environmental dangers and more positive effects of therapeutic programming and to better prepare the juveniles for release back into the community. These coefficients are all statistically significant at the .05 level. However, these models further indicate that the current models are not the best fit to the data. According to each models' χ^2, significant variation across the facilities' means remains. This finding suggests the addition of covariates into the hierarchical linear model.

I have displayed the results from the full model in two tables (Table 11 and Table 12). Table 11 displays the beta coefficients for the effect of the facility characteristics (listed across the top of the table) on the thirteen conditions of confinement (listed in the first column of the table). The primary variable of interest, the operating sector, is located in column two. The absolute values of the operating sector coefficients range from .01 to .16 with none of the coefficients reaching the .05 level of statistical significance. As compared to the earlier model, these coefficients are no longer statistically significant once the model controls other facility characteristics.

The results from this model address the third question in this study: Are the conditions of confinement perceived to be more favorable in private or public facilities by the juveniles and the staff? From the staff perspective, controlling for the characteristics of the facilities and the individual characteristics of the correctional staff, there are no statistically significant differences in the conditions of confinement between public and private facilities.

Facility Level Covariates. As with the juvenile models, these staff perception models provide insights into other factors that impact perceptions of conditions of confinement. Table 11 outlines the unstandardized beta coefficients for all other facility level variables included in the models for each of the thirteen conditions of confinement. Three variables that demonstrated a strong impact on staff perceptions of the conditions were the facility's capacity, the availability of follow-up information and the type of program.

Staff perceived that larger facilities had a more negative environment with significantly less control, activity, care, quality of life and justice. They also perceived the therapeutic programs to be less beneficial and the juveniles to be less prepared for release. Further, staff perceived larger facilities had higher levels of environmental dangers and risks to residents. Recall, from the discussion of impact of capacity in the juvenile models that despite the apparent magnitude of these coefficients, the scale of capacity is based on the addition of one person to the facility, and thus the effects are substantive.

Another interesting finding is the consistent statistical significance of the availability of follow-up information about the juveniles who leave the facilities. Similar to the results from the juvenile models, staff in facilities that collected or received follow up information perceived the environment to have higher levels of control, activity, care, quality of life, structure, and justice. Further they perceived that the facility's therapeutic programming is more effective and the juveniles are better prepared to transition back into the community. Lastly, they perceived less danger from all sources, fewer risks to residents and residents have less freedom in their daily activities. The absolute values of the beta coefficients for this variable range from .10 to .38 and are significant in eight of the thirteen conditions of confinement.

As expected, significant differences were also demonstrated in the staff perceptions of the conditions of confinement depending upon the type of program. The most consistent and significant differences existed between detention centers and other types of programs. The staff that worked in detention centers perceived these facilities to have more negative conditions of confinement as compared to other programs. Staff perceived that detention centers had low levels of control, activity, care, quality of life, structure, and justice. The staff also perceived that they had poor therapeutic programming and failed to adequately prepare the juveniles for release into the community. Further, they had higher levels of danger from all sources, more risks to residents and more freedom.

Individual Level Covariates. I have outlined the unstandardized beta coefficients from the effects of the individual characteristics of the staff members on their perceptions of the conditions of confinement in Table 12. Two individual level variables were found to have a strong impact on the staff perceptions of the conditions of confinement: age, and current length of employment.

Despite the small magnitude of the age of the staff coefficients, they were statistically significantly for a number of the conditions of confinement including the perceived level of activity, care, quality of life, structure and all sources of danger. As the age of staff members increased, they perceived a lower level of activity, and danger from all sources. Further, the older the staff member the higher levels of perceived care, quality of life and structure. Additionally, staff who had been employed by the facilities for a longer period of time viewed the environment as having less control, more danger from all sources and more freedom.

Conclusion. From the perspective of both the juvenile delinquents who live and the correctional staff whom the correctional facilities employ, the conditions of confinement between private and public correctional facilities were not statistically significantly different when controlling for facility and individual level characteristics.

Impact of Operating Sector on Juvenile Adjustment

The fourth question of this study asked: Do privately operated correctional facilities differentially impact the adjustment of juveniles? To investigate the change in juvenile adjustment measures, I used only a subset of the total sample (n=530) who were administered the survey at both Time 1 and Time 2. The time between the two measurement periods varied by facility, ranging from three months to eight months. For some of the facilities, this time period coincided with the program length capturing the juveniles upon admission into the facility and completion of the program. For other juveniles, this time period was random holding no specific meaning. Five measures of adjustment were considered: pro-social attitudes, anxiety, dysfunctional impulsivity, depression, and social bonds. As described previously, the first three scales ranged between 1 and 2, the depression and social bond scales ranged from one to five.

To begin the comparisons, the initial levels of adjustment at the first administration were considered. I used a nested analysis-of-variance model to test for differences between private and public facilities. As shown in Table 13, results demonstrated that juveniles held in private facilities self-reported significantly lower levels of depression, dysfunctional impulsivity, and higher levels of social bonds to family, school and work as compared to juveniles in public facilities.

Additionally, I compared the levels of the adjustment variables measured at the time of the second survey administration. The nested analysis of variance models demonstrated that at this latter point in time juveniles in private facilities reported less depression and stronger social bonds as compared with juveniles in public facilities. Further, juveniles in private facilities reported higher levels of pro-social attitudes than juveniles in public facilities.

From these cross sectional viewpoints, it appeared that juveniles in private facilities adjust more positively. For a clearer understanding of adjustment that occurred over time, I calculated change scores. I formed the change scores by subtracting the time 1 score from the time 2 score. Thus, a resulting positive change score indicated an increase in the adjustment variable. This was a desirable result for the pro-social attitudes and social bond variables but undesirable for the depression, anxiety and dysfunctional impulsivity variables. For example, if an individual's social bond score at time one was 3.5, and the social bonds score at time two was

4.0 (e.g., 4.0 - 3.5 = .5), the resulting positive change score (.5) indicated an increase in the individual's social bonds over time. Additionally, if an individual's depression scores at time one was 3.0 and at time two was 4.0 (e.g., 4.0 - 3.0 = 1), the resulting positive change score indicated an increase in the individual's level of depression over time.

In summary, it would be ideal to see change scores that are positive for pro-social attitudes and social bonds, and negative change scores for depression, anxiety and dysfunctional impulsivity. Table 14 outlines the change scores by operating sector.

As expected, the results demonstrated larger change scores in the variables that had a broader scale range. The absolute values of the scores in scales that ranged from 1 to 2 are between .008 and .189. The change scores of the scales that had a range of 1 to 5 were .005 and .209 (absolute values).

When I applied the nested analysis-of-variance model to these change scores, the results indicated the amount of change between private and public facilities was statistically significant for two of the five adjustment variables. Pro-social attitudes increased for juveniles in private correctional facilities and decreased for juveniles in public facilities. Levels of dysfunctional impulsivity decreased for juveniles in both private and public facilities.

To gain confidence in these indications of change, it was necessary to control for individual characteristics and facility characteristics that may impact changes in these outcomes. Following the modeling strategy used in examining the impact of the operating sector on environmental perceptions, I implemented a hierarchical linear model in progressive steps. To begin with, I used individual characteristics of the juveniles to predict the change scores for each of the adjustment variables.

Results demonstrated that the adjustment model for depression indicated that the individual characteristics of the juveniles explained all the variation across facility means. Specifically, the juvenile delinquent's lengths of sentence and their type of offense were significant predictors of change in depression levels. Juveniles who had longer sentences were more likely to experience change in depression while juveniles convicted of property offenses experienced less change in depression.

Results from the remaining four adjustment models demonstrated that sufficient variation across the facilities' means to allow for exploration of the impact of operating sector and other covariates. Thus, the next step was to incorporate the impact of the operating sector in the second level of the hierarchical model.

Table 15 displays the coefficients for the effect of the operating sector on each of the four remaining adjustment variables in row 2. Note that I have listed the covariates in Column 1 while I have listed the adjustment variables across the top of Row 1. The results from the adjustment models indicated the operating sector significantly impacts change in the juveniles' social bonds. Juveniles in private facilities experienced a greater decrease in their levels of social bonds (adjusted change score = -.267) than juveniles in public facilities who experience a less dramatic decrease in social bonds (adjusted change score = -.051).

The operating sector did not significantly impact any of the other changes in adjustment variables. However, significant variation remained across the means of the facilities to warrant further exploration as indicated by a significant χ^2 in the remaining models. Consequently, a number of facility level covariates were added to the model such that it was comparable to the full model previously utilized in exploring conditions of confinement. In addition to the typical facility level variables, a measure of the quality of the conditions of confinement was added. The variable, Perceived Environment, is a scale score ranging from one to five, which was based on the juveniles' perceptions of conditions of confinement at the first survey administration[10].

---

[10] The conditions of confinement items factor analyzed into one factor, however, for interpretation and consistency with previous research I had divided the items into

I have displayed the results from the full model in Table 16. Controlling for the individual level characteristics and facility level characteristics, a significant new development became evident. While the operating sector continued to be a significant predictor of juveniles' change in social bonds, it became a significant predictor of anxiety. The coefficients demonstrated that juveniles in private facilities significantly decreased in their level of social bonds (adjusted change score = -.333) between the survey administrations. Contrary to the unadjusted change score, juveniles in public facilities decreased in their levels of social bonds (adjusted change score = -.039), however, the decrease in bonds was much greater for juveniles in private facilities.

Further, results demonstrated that juveniles in private facilities reported a significant increase in their level of anxiety while juveniles in public facilities experienced a significant decrease in anxiety. However, the operating sector did not have a significant impact on the juveniles' change in pro-social attitudes, or reported levels of dysfunctional impulsivity.

These results showed that juveniles in private facilities experienced more negative adjustment between survey administrations, especially as indicated by the change in their levels of anxiety and social bonds. However, the substantive size of change is small and thus surprisingly few differences exist between the juvenile delinquents. Additionally, these findings must be considered alongside a caution. Recall that the adjustment scales ranged from either one to two, or, one to five. Thus, there was an upper limit to each of the scales. Recall that the exploration of the level of adjustment outcomes at time of the first survey administration indicated that juveniles in private facilities were very high on the social bond scale (M = 3.67). It is possible that the effect demonstrated in the model of social bonds was due to a "ceiling effect."

---

the thirteen scales when used as dependent variables in the previous models.

That is, the reasonable explanation for the decrease in the social bonds in private facilities is not that the facilities fail to promote an environment for positive growth but that the juveniles were likely to regress to the mean based on their initial scores.

In summary, the changes that occurred in the brief time period between survey administrations were most likely attributable to a "ceiling effect", an artifact of the scales as opposed to any true differences in the scores. Given this potential for statistical artifacts, the most informative data on juvenile adjustment allowed within these data were examinations of the initial levels of the adjustment variables and differences therein.

Impact of Operating Sector on Staff Work Experiences

The final question that I will address is: Do privately operated correctional facilities differentially impact the work experiences of the correctional staff? To answer this question, I have included four measures of staff work experiences: staff communication, level of stress, job satisfaction, and staff support. Responses were based on a five-point scale with higher scores indicative of higher levels of the variables. The means of the staff work experiences were grouped by operating sector and presented in Table 17.

Means differences were tested using the nested analysis-of-variance models. Results demonstrated that all four of the self reported work experience measures were statistically significantly different between private and public facilities at the .05 level of significance. Thus, compared to correctional staff in public facilities, the correctional staff employed in private facilities perceived their environment to be a more positive work environment and experienced less stress.

The next step was to determine the extent to which various facility characteristics and individual characteristics contributed to these differences in work experiences. Consequently, I implemented a hierarchical linear model approach. Initially, I only entered the individual characteristics of the staff into the HLM models to determine whether sufficient variation remained across facilities means. Results from the level-1 models found that variation did remain across the facility means to warrant the exploration of the impact of facility level characteristics on perceived work experiences.

The characteristics of the facility were added at the second level of the model in addition to the individual characteristics, which existed at the first level. The second level of the model included the facility variables that I have utilized in previous models. Additionally, I included a composite measure of the perceived conditions of confinement by the staff (Perceived Environment) as a single factor score that consisted of all the questions from the thirteen environmental scales[11].

I have displayed results from these models in Table 18. The variables that were included at the second level (facility level) of the model are listed in uppercase with the individual characteristics at level 1 listed in lowercase for each of the work experience measures. The full HLM model demonstrated consistency across the four work experience measures. I have listed the primary variable of interest, the operating sector, in the Row 1 of Table 18. The coefficients, ranging from .018 to .106, demonstrated that operating sector had no significant impact on any of the four work experience outcomes. That is, the operating sector did not differentially impact the work experiences of the correctional staff between private and public correctional facilities.

However, a number of other factors demonstrated a significant impact on staff work experience. At the facility level, staff members

---

[11]The conditions of confinement items analyzed into one factor, however, for interpretation and consistency with previous research I had divided the items into the thirteen scales when used as dependent variables in the previous models.

who were employed by facilities that had a more intensive admission process reported lower stress levels. Additionally, the larger the juvenile to staff ratios at a facility, results demonstrated higher stress levels of the correctional staff. Interestingly, the type of program (e.g., boot camp, detention center etc.) did not have an impact on the staff work experiences when controlling for these other factors.

The most consistent and significant finding at the facility level was the impact of the perceived conditions of confinement on all four measures of staff work experiences. If the staff perceived the correctional facility to have positive conditions of confinement, they were also more likely to report higher levels of staff communication, job satisfaction and support of the staff as well as lower levels of stress. However, it is important to recall that staff reported their perceptions and experiences were measured during the same survey administration, unlike the juvenile reported perceptions and adjustment. Thus, it is unclear whether the positive work experiences were a result of the perceived positive environment, and conversely negative work experiences (stress, perceived lack of staff communication and staff support, as well as lack of job satisfaction) were a result of the perceived negative work environment. The alternative is that an unsatisfied employee felt stressed and projected negative feelings onto their perceptions of the workplace conditions of confinement.

The results of the model also demonstrated some interesting findings at the individual level. Age, the length of current employment, race and to some extent the level of education all had consistent effects on the staff members' work experience. Younger correctional staff reported more staff communication, job satisfaction, staff support and less stress than older staff members. Further, staff that the facility has employed for a longer period of time reported significantly less staff communication and support, and more stress.

Significant differences also appeared between white and nonwhite correctional staff. Coefficients demonstrated that minority staff members perceived work experiences to be more negative. I have coded this model race as white (1) and non white (0), thus, the coefficients suggest that minorities perceive less staff communication, job satisfaction, and support as well as experiencing more stress. These coefficients range from .157 to .222 and were all statistically significant at the .05 level.

These findings are cause for concern given their consistency across all work experience measures. Follow up studies should investigate whether these findings are due to differences in perceptions of the work environment or due to a more serious problem of inequality in the workplace.

The focus of these models was to determine whether the staff perceived work experiences in private and public facilities to be significantly different. Results demonstrated that although the operating sector did not impact staff work experiences, some facility and individual covariates, such as the perception of the conditions of confinement in the environment, and race were important predictors of work experiences.

Conclusion. This study has found that there were no significant differences in the perceived environmental quality between private and public juvenile correctional facilities. Further, the operating sector did not give rise to substantive differences in the adjustment of the juvenile delinquents or the work experiences of the correctional staff that the facilities employ. Private and public facilities have both been embedded in the same criminal justice system since the inception of the juvenile correctional facility and it may be as a result of this historical coexistence that the concerns of privatization critics were unfounded.

One consideration however that needs to be made is the difference in the characteristics of the facilities and correctional staff between private and public facilities. Comparisons of descriptive characteristics suggested that private facilities were distinctly newer, smaller and more intensive in their admission procedure. Further, the private facilities were found to employ younger, inexperienced correctional staff. These findings led me to postulate that the operating sector may have an indirect effect on environmental quality as detailed in Figure 2 that could be tested in future research.

CHAPTER 7

Discussion

The exponential growth of private industry in the operation of correctional facilities in the past decade has attracted the attention of both researchers and practitioners. Opponents to privatization argue that the profit seeking nature of private corporations may compromise the quality of privately operated facilities. They argue private correctional facilities would be more likely to have minimal provision of goods and services, hire inexperienced staff and skim the offender population to be more cost effective and this will result in compromised environmental quality. Supporters of privatization suggest the private sector could do no worse than the quality of the conditions that currently exist in public correctional facilities. In their opinion, the newer staff could breathe new life into the facilities, since less experienced staff may be more innovative and fluid in their thinking when issues arise. Further, given that private juvenile correctional facilities have coexisted since the inception of facilities for juveniles, I did not expect to find drastic differences between the two environments.

In this study, I utilized data from 48 facilities in 19 states to empirically explore five questions. Included in the exploration were comparisons of the demographic composition of the juvenile delinquent population, the correctional staff and characteristics of the facility. I also compared the perceived quality of the conditions of confinement between the two types of facilities from the perspective of both the juvenile delinquents and the correctional staff. Lastly, I examined the impact of the operating sector on the adjustment of the juvenile delinquents and the work experiences of the staff.

The initial analyses considered differences in the demographic composition of the juvenile delinquents. Results demonstrated the juvenile delinquents held in private facilities were not substantively different from those held in public facilities on demographic indicators and scales that measured criminogenic risk factors. They only statistically significant differences between the samples were that private facilities held more males and more juvenile delinquents incarcerated as a result of a property offense.

Demographic characteristics of the staff that the correctional facilities employed as well as their background experiences were also examined. Statistical comparisons demonstrated that staff employed in the private facilities were significantly younger, had less prior experience in correctional facilities and were employed for a shorter period of time. The lack of experience and short record of employment of the majority of the staff employed in private facilities is one explanation for the common argument that employees in private facilities receive a lower salary with fewer benefits as compared to public facility employees.

Finally, comparisons of facility characteristics between private and public correctional facilities demonstrated that as compared to public facilities, private facilities were significantly smaller, newer and had a more intensive admission process for juvenile delinquents. This finding supported the conclusions drawn earlier by Bartollas (1997) that private facilities are less often high security and more frequently smaller, non-secure facilities holding a limited number of delinquents. Thus, private facilities operate different types of facility than those operated by the public sector.

Turning to the juvenile delinquent and staff perceptions of the conditions of confinement, I explored difference in the mean levels of conditions of confinement between private and public correctional facilities. Initially, I did not include controls for the characteristics of the facilities, staff or juvenile delinquents. Based on both the perceptions of the staff and juveniles, results demonstrated that differences between the conditions of confinement in private and public correctional facilities were not statistically significant.

In further analysis of the quality of the environment, I included covariates for the facility characteristics as well as individual characteristics of the staff or juvenile delinquents by implementing a hierarchical linear model. This more complex model added a limitation to the findings. Given the limited number of facilities in the study (n=48), the degrees of freedom at the level 2 of the model were reduced to a small number once I included the facility level covariates. The limited degrees of freedom may have affected the statistical significance of the coefficients such that they were less likely to demonstrate significance.

Results from the full models, which included the individual and facility level covariates, found that there were no statistically significant differences in the perceived conditions of confinement between private and public facilities. Not only were there no significant differences between private and public facilities on a large number of indicators of the environment, the perceptions of the juvenile delinquents and the correctional staff were strikingly similar. One might expect that juvenile delinquents who are confined by the courts to these facilities would have a very different view of their environment as compared to staff members who chose to work in the facility. Despite this expectation, the perceptions from these two different data sources were highly correlated. The similarity between juveniles and staff perceptions added confidence and reliability to the conclusion that there were no significant differences in the environmental quality of private and public correctional facilities.

In summarizing the relationship between the operating sector of juvenile correctional facilities and the environmental quality the above results alluded to a more complex relationship when considered together. Through these analyses, I identified that the operating sector did impact some individual and facility level characteristics. That is, private facilities were significantly different from public facilities on variables such as size, age of facility, age of correctional staff and so forth. Tables 2, 3 and 4 displayed these statistically significant differences. Although the operating sector did not directly impact the environmental quality, as indicated in Tables 7, 8, 11 and 12 some of these facility and individual differences were found to have a statistically significant impact on the conditions of confinement. These findings suggest that the operating sector may have an indirect effect on the conditions of confinement. That is, the operating sector impacted the characteristics of the facility and the individuals (see Figure 2).

In addition to considering differences between private and public correctional facilities, I also considered whether privately operated correctional facilities differentially impacted on the juvenile delinquents' adjustment. The findings from the examination of juvenile adjustment were not as clear as the differences in environmental quality. Results demonstrated that juveniles in private facilities experienced a statistically significant increase in their level of anxiety and decrease in the level of social bonds but these differences were substantively small. Thus, it appeared that there were limited differences between public and private facilities in their impact on juvenile adjustment. However, the results from the social bonds model lack confidence because there was a serious methodological limitation of the scale due a "ceiling effect". It was possible that these statistically significant findings were due to a statistical artifact of the scales used to measure the levels of social bonds. Future research on the adjustment of juveniles may wish to consider an alternative means of measuring these factors that does not lend itself to the possibility of a "ceiling effect." For example, using indicators of social bonds in addition to attitudinal measures such as observational study of parent-juvenile interactions or a measure with a higher top end that is more differentiated scale.

The impact of the operating sector on the correctional staff work experiences was also somewhat unclear. Results indicated that the operating sector did not significantly impact any one of the four measures of staff work experiences. However, the operating sector may have had an indirect impact. The strongest predictor of staff work experiences was the perceived environment. Recall that Figure 2 suggested the operating sector impacted the facility and individual level factors that in turn impacted the perceptions of the conditions of confinement. It is possible to take this indirect effect one step further to include conditions of confinement impacting staff work experiences as suggested by the results. However, since the correctional staff had only been surveyed at one time period, their work experiences could have affected their perceptions of the environment instead of the relationship postulated above. I do not expect that one factor would have a mutually exclusive impact on the other. It is more plausible that simultaneity between the variables exists.

In addition to addressing the main questions examined in this study, these analyses provided insight into a number of important issues that should be considered in future research. First, this study found support for a mixed model of importation and deprivation factors in the adjustment of juvenile delinquents. Secondly, it found differences in the perceptions of conditions of confinement based on an individual's race and their history of family violence and child abuse. Finally, this study found the availability of follow-up information on juvenile delinquents was a significant indicator of the environmental conditions of confinement.

In the models that considered differences in environmental quality based on juvenile and staff perception, a number of the individual and facility level covariates significantly predicted the quality of the conditions of confinement as discussed earlier. The significance of these covariates addresses two bodies of literature, importation and deprivation studies. Recall, that these areas of the literature respectively argue that an offender's experiences are a result of individual characteristics that they "import" into the correctional facility or are a result of factors within the correctional facility environment. These results support a mixed model of importation and deprivation in that both individual and facility characteristics were important in the juveniles' experiences in the correctional facilities.

In examining both the staff and juvenile delinquent's perceptions of the correctional facility's conditions of confinement, minority participants' perceptions were found to be significantly more negative than the Caucasian participants' perceptions. This finding was statistically significant for juvenile perceptions across both the negative and positive conditions of confinement which indicated that not only did minority juvenile delinquents perceive the environment to have higher levels of danger but they also perceived fewer benefits from the therapeutic programming and less prepared for release. Interestingly, the staff perceptions coincided with the juvenile perceptions. Minority staff members also perceived the environment to be more dangerous, less caring and so forth.

The question that this study cannot answer is whether these perceived differences are due to perceptual differences or unequal treatment of minorities in correctional facilities. That is, minorities may interpret the environment differently from non-minorities despite equality of treatment. Alternatively and more plausibly, minorities may be treated differently in these correctional environments. If the latter explanation is true, I expect that minority juveniles are more frequently teased and challenged by other juvenile delinquents and correctional staff. This would have led the minority juvenile delinquents to perceive their environment as more dangerous from other resident and staff and to be less caring. Treatment approaches and transitional programming may not have been directed in a manner that minority juveniles could relate to and thus minority juvenile delinquents perceived the therapeutic programming as less beneficial and felt unprepared for release. This finding is cause for concern and should be considered more directly by future research.

The analyses in this study also demonstrated differences in perceptions by individuals who have a history of family violence and child abuse. Results demonstrated that individuals with a more extensive history of abuse perceived the environment as having more danger, less control, less structure. They also perceived fewer benefits from the therapeutic programming and felt unprepared for release. Thus, the environments of these correctional facilities and the types of therapeutic programming are not targeting the needs of this abused portion of the population. If one of our goals in the juvenile justice system is to rehabilitate juvenile delinquents to become productive members of society, we should reconsider the assignment of seriously abused juveniles into programs that do not focus on healing the psychological, emotional and sometimes physical scars produced by the juvenile delinquents' history.

Another consistent finding was the significance of the follow-up information variable on a number of conditions of confinement. However, its impact on the conditions of confinement was unclear. One possibility is a facility that obtains follow up information on juveniles is better able to determine the success and impact of their program and adjust therapeutic components accordingly. Thus, the availability of this information creates a feedback loop between the outcomes and the facility's therapeutic components. The difficulty with this explanation is that most therapeutic programs are not so malleable that they can be easily adjusted multiple times per year based on feedback statistics. It is more likely that the implementation of therapeutic components in the facilities is based on the findings available in the criminological and psychological literature from large-scale studies completed by evaluation researchers.

Another explanation is that the existence of follow-up information acts as a proxy for a "quality" correctional facility. An administrator who optimally staffs and operates their facility is likely to have a researcher who is able to collect or obtain follow-up information such as recidivism statistics. At the very minimum, if the facility is without research support, a quality correctional facility would be concerned with obtaining some external evaluation of the outcomes of their program on which they might base their success. However, it may be that administrators ensure this information is compiled because of contractual requirements or merit-based systems. Thus, not all facilities may be collecting this information with the goal of improving their facility.

Implication for Policy and Research

Based on the results from this national evaluation, we know that the majority of private facilities are smaller and newer facilities that often operate programs other than detention centers and training schools with younger, less experienced staff. We also know that public and private facilities do not have statistically significant differences in environmental quality when similar facilities are compared. Thus, does utility exist for the privatization of juvenile correctional facilities? If we only consider the issue of quality, based on this evidence we can argue that private correctional facilities do not necessarily add or detract to the environmental quality.

I have discussed a number of other concerns about privatization in the literature including (1) the philosophical debate regarding punishment ideologies (DiIulio, 1988, 1991; Logan 1990), and, (2) the economic viability of private facilities. Although this study has provided insight on the quality issue, the moral stances on the appropriateness or inappropriateness of private corporations punishing citizens will remain. This philosophical issue does not lend itself to empirical testing, only to discussions and debate. On the other hand, the cost effectiveness of privatization does allow for empirical testing, though it may be a challenging task.

The most conclusive evidence provided to date is an examination of cost effectiveness using meta-analytic techniques as mentioned in an earlier chapter. Pratt and Maahs (1997) concluded that private correctional facilities were no more cost effective than public correctional facilities. Instead, other institutional characteristics such as the facility's economy of scale, age and security level were the strongest predictor's of the offender's per diem costs. Thus, empirical evidence has demonstrated that private correctional facilities are neither more cost effective nor of better quality than public correctional facilities.

However, one of the areas ripe for the cost cutting knives in private correctional facilities is therapeutic programming. There is limited attention allocated to the success rate of these programs in relation to recidivism rates and rehabilitation of offenders. The private sector has no cause to focus on programming and other rehabilitation tools if no one holds them accountable for these aspects. If this is the case, then such programming would not be a priority of privatized facilities. There has not been systematic empirical research that compares private and government run correctional facilities in terms of long term impact on offenders (e.g., recidivism, return to work).

If there are limited differences between public and private correctional facilities in terms of quality and cost effectiveness, why might we expect differences in long-term impact on offenders? Recall some of the characteristics of private facilities from Table 4. A large number of private facilities (50%) collected or obtained follow up information on the juveniles whom staff released from their facilities as compared to 34% of public facilities. This collection of evaluative information addresses one the major deficiencies noted in reviews of rehabilitation programs which is the lack of systematic and thorough evaluation practices (Gendreau & Goggin, 1997). Gendreau and Goggin suggest that a more successful program will systematically collect information on offenders and have regularly scheduled evaluations of their program.

Of equal importance in impacting recidivism and rehabilitation of the juvenile delinquents are characteristics of the programs. Private facilities are smaller programs that contain fewer delinquents at one time with a more intensive admission process. An intensive admission process allows for a more detailed evaluation of the individual juveniles. Consequently, the treatment staff at these facilities may be more prepared to identify and address the delinquent's level of risks and needs in private facilities. Gendreau and Goggin (1997) also suggested that an intensive process of evaluation, such as this, is one part of addressing the "risk principle" that is necessary for achieving effective rehabilitation.

Thus, although private facilities do not seem to provide either a superior environmental quality or tremendous cost effectiveness as compared to public facilities, they may hold potential for a more positive long-term impact on delinquents. This is one avenue that researchers should explore further in the immediate future. More specifically, evaluators should monitor and compare the types of programs offered by private facilities and the treatment quality, quantity and integrity. Researchers should further examine differences in the training and qualifications of the treatment personnel. Additionally, given the expansion of the private sector into areas such as electronic monitoring, the aftercare and transitional assistance into the community must be considered since all of these factors are important in determining the effectiveness of a program in rehabilitating offenders.

In conclusion, although we need to maintain accountability of the conditions of confinement in private correctional facilities as with public facilities, we can be more comfortable knowing that the environmental quality of private facilities is not significantly different from the quality of conditions in public facilities. From this point, criminological researchers need to focus beyond the issue of quality of the environment and turn towards outcome evaluations and the long-term effects of incarceration in private correctional facilities. It is only once empirical evidence is able to inform us about all of these aspects and impacts of privatization, that we can recommend the operation of correctional facilities by private corporations.

Table 1: Comparison of Conditions of Confinement Models, page 1

Factor	Prison Quality Index	Prison Environment Inventory	Correctional Facilities Environment Scale
1	Security	Privacy	Staff control
2	Activity	Activity Social Stimulation	Involvement
3	Safety	Safety	
4	Justice		Clarity
5	Order	Structure	Order Organization
6	Conditions		
7	Care	Emotional feedback Support	Expressiveness Support Personal problems Orientation
8	Management & problems		
9			Freedom
10			

Table 1: Comparison of Conditions of Confinement Models (continued)

Factor	OJJDP Conditions of Confinement	Bureau of Prison's Prison Social Climate Survey
1	Security arrangements	Security
2		Services
3	Staffing, deaths Health care issues	Personal Safety
4		
5		
6		Quality of Life Personal well-being
7		
8		
9	Autonomy	Community access
10	Practical Orientation	

Table 2: Demographic Description of Juvenile Sample

Demographic Characteristic	Private Facilities		Public Facilities			
	%	N	%		N	
Gender (% male)*	97.1	1157	92.2		2559	
Race						
Non-White	61.6	734	70.5		1942	
White	38.4	457	29.6		815	
Offense						
Person	21.5	256	23.7		658	
Property*	34.2	407	25.0		695	
Drug	14.0	166	13.4		371	
Other	22.5	268	28.4		789	
	M	SD	N	M	SD	N
Age (yrs.)	16.2	1.30	1186	16.2	1.2	2767
Sentence length (mos.)	9.1	10.30	1125	12.6	18.9	2323
Time in facility (mos.)	3.7	4.60	1151	4.2	6.2	2659
Alcohol abuse	1.34	.31	1183	1.32	.31	2743
Drug abuse	1.47	.33	1184	1.44	.33	2743
Family violence / child abuse	1.56	.63	1181	1.61	.70	2726
Age at 1st arrest	13.40	2.00	1148	13.3	2.1	2698
Previous commitments	2.40	2.20	1146	2.9	2.0	2647

Table 3: Demographic Description of Staff Sample

Demographic Characteristic		Private Facilities			Public Facilities		
		%	N		%	N	
Gender (% male)		61.3	447		67.9	887	
Race	Non-White	37.9	262		36.7	319	
	White	62.2	273		63.3	551	
Education Level	Graduate school	22.9	102		23.3	205	
	College degree	32.8	146		33.0	290	
	Some college	27.9	124		28.9	254	
	High school	16.2	72		14.9	131	
		M	SD	N	M	SD	N
Age (yrs)*		34.2	9.6	428	39.4	10.2	838
Previous correctional employment (yrs)*		1.09	2.9	421	1.72	4.1	841
Length of employment at current facility (yrs)*		1.89	2.4	437	5.76	6.7	854

Note: Categorical differences tested using a random effects probit model. Mean difference tested using a nested analysis-of-variance, with facilities nested within facility type. $p < .05$

Table 4: Description of Facilities

Characteristic	Private Facilities			Public Facilities		
	%	N		%	N	
Type of Program						
Boot Camp	68.8	11		40.6	13	
Detention Center	0	0		12.5	4	
Training School	6.3	1		25.0	8	
Other	25.0	4		21.9	7	
Regional Location						
North	6.3	1		9.4	3	
East	18.8	3		34.4	11	
Midwest	37.5	6		12.5	4	
West	0	0		15.6	5	
South	37.5	6		28.1	9	
Follow up data (% yes)	50	8		34.4	11	
	M	SD	N	M	SD	N
Maximum Capacity*	60.4	38.6	16	134.4	137	32
Age of Facility (years)*	4.4	4.2	16	29.6	37.7	32
Admission Process Index*	.56	.23	16	.40	.29	32
Population Seriousness Index	1.15	.48	16	1.29	.49	32
Juvenile-Staff ratio	3.09	6.6	16	1.70	3.13	32
Visitation Hrs./week	5.11	3.1	16	5.63	5.0	32

Note: Mean difference tested using t-tests. $p < .05$

Table 5: Juvenile Perceptions of Conditions of Confinement (Raw means)

Environmental Condition		Private Facilities			Public Facilities		
		M	SD	N	M	SD	N
Positive Conditions							
	Control	3.74	.75	1159	3.62	.75	2629
	Activity	3.97	.82	1142	3.72	.90	2575
	Care	3.37	.79	1140	3.20	.70	2568
	Quality of Life	2.97	.69	1139	2.95	.69	2552
	Structure	3.73	.73	1136	3.67	.71	2541
	Justice	3.13	.82	1135	3.05	.75	2530
	Therapeutic programs	3.55	.99	1131	3.46	1.0	2529
	Preparation for release	3.89	.70	1180	3.80	.72	2738
Negative Conditions							
	Resident Danger	2.00	.83	1152	2.27	.81	2628
	Danger from Staff	2.46	1.1	1143	2.38	1.0	2607
	Environmental Danger	2.51	.98	1141	2.80	.94	2578
	Risks to Residents	2.40	.84	1151	2.47	.86	2575
	Freedom	2.09	.72	1132	2.34	.78	2535

Table 6: The Effects of Operating Sector and Individual Level Covariates on Juvenile Perceptions of Conditions of Confinement (B)

Condition of Confinement	Operating Sector (B)	p
Positive Conditions		
Control	.10	.41
Activity	.23*	.05
Care	.14	.23
Quality of Life	-.00	.98
Structure	.03	.76
Justice	.05	.60
Therapeutic Programs	.10	.43
Preparation for Release	.08	.14
Negative Conditions		
Resident Danger	-.18	.19
Danger from Staff	.06	.73
Environmental Danger	-.18	.26
Risks to Residents	-.03	.80
Freedom	-.17	.14

Note: Operating sector is coded Private = 1and Public = 0.
$p < .05$

Table 7: The Effects of Facility Level Characteristics on Juvenile Perceptions of Conditions of Confinement (B), page 1

Condition of Confinement (DV)	Operating sector	Admission process index	Serious	Follow up data	Age
Positive conditions					
Control	-.21	.41	-.05	.26*	-.001
Activity	.02	.22	-.13	.22*	-.001
Care	-.04	.26	.01	.26*	-.002
Quality of Life	-.13	-.19	-.02	.17	-.003
Structure	-.19*	.18	-.02	.20*	-.004*
Justice	-.06	.17	.11	.17	-.002
Therapeutic Prog.	-.10	.18	-.12	.15	-.001
Prep. for Release	.02	.15	-.02	.09	-.001
Negative conditions					
Resident Danger	.17	-.43	-.02	-.18	.002
Danger from Staff	.11	-.64	-.22	-.54*	-.001
Environ. Danger	.17	-.51	.09	-.33*	-.0009
Risks to Residents	.22	-.23	.05	-.33*	.002
Freedom	.10	-.41	-.02	.01	-.0008

* $p < .05$

Table 7: The Effects of Facility Level Characteristics on Juvenile Perceptions of Conditions of Confinement (B), page 2

Condition of Confinement (DV)	Capacity	Juvenile-staff ratio	Type of Program		
			Boot camp	Detention center	Training school
Positive conditions					
Control	-.0002	-.01	.14	-.50*	-.06
Activity	-.0009	-.01	-.03	-.58*	-.04
Care	-.0009	-.02	-.11	-.58*	-.11
Quality of Life	-.0008	-.01	-.13	-.54*	-.24
Structure	-.0003	-.01	.00	-.55*	-.03
Justice	-.0010*	-.02*	-.20	-.48*	-.15
Therapeutic Prog.	-.0009	-.02	-.04	-.69*	-.14
Prep. for Release	-.0002	-.01	-.03	-.06	-.04
Negative conditions					
Resident Danger	.0008	-.004	-.19	.42	-.05
Danger from Staff	.0012	.03	.41	.19	.47
Environ. Danger	.0009	-.001	-.06	.80*	.78
Risks to Residents	.0011*	.01	-.07	.49*	.02
Freedom	-.0004	-.02*	-.39*	.05	-.005

Table 7: The Effects of Facility Level Characteristics on Juvenile Perceptions of Conditions of Confinement (B), page 3

Condition of Confinement (DV)	No. of visiting hours	Region		
		N	E	M
Positive Conditions				
Control	-.02	-.09	.10	.11
Activity	-.03*	.31	.33*	.12
Care	-.02	.26	.42*	.14
Quality of Life	-.01	.25	.31*	.08
Structure	-.01	.13	.32*	.18
Justice	-.01	.10	.25*	.04
Therapeutic Prog.	-.03*	.29	.19	-.07
Prep. for Release	-.004	-.10	.11	-.06
Negative Conditions				
Resident Danger	.01	-.21	-.23	-.30
Danger from Staff	-.03	-.25	-.34	-.28
Environ. Danger	.02	-.42*	-.35*	-.19
Risks to Residents	.02	-.16	-.15	-.02
Freedom	-.003	.22	.25	-.15

Table 8: The Effects of Individual Level Juvenile Characteristics on Juvenile Perceptions of Conditions of Confinement (B), page 1

Condition of Confinement (DV) Confinement (DV)	Age	Gender	Race	Sentence length
Positive Conditions				
Control	-.00	-.02*	.05	.00
Activity	-.03*	.01	.06	.00
Care	-.03*	-.07	.03	.00
Quality of Life	-.05	.09	.00	-.00
Structure	-.01	-.02	.08*	-.00
Justice	-.01	-.10	.12*	-.00
Therapeutic Prog.	-.05*	.03	-.10*	.00
Prep. for Release	-.01	-.12	.03	.00
Negative Conditions				
Resident Danger	-.04*	.20*	.00	.00
Danger from Staff	-.02	.17	-.10*	-.00
Environ. Danger	.02	.08	-.10*	.00
Risks to Residents	.01	.02	-.13*	.002*
Freedom	-.00	.17*	-.04	.00

p<.05

Table 8: The Effects of Individual Level Juvenile Characteristics on Juvenile Perceptions of Conditions of Confinement (B), page 2

Conditions of Confinement (DV)	Time in program	Age at 1st arrest	Number of prior commitments	child abuse
Positive Conditions				
Control				
Activity	-.01*	.02*	-.01	-.08*
Care	-.00	.02*	.00	-.08*
Quality of Life	.01	.02*	.00	-.11*
Structure	.00	.07	-.00	-.06*
Justice	-.00	.02*	.00	-.05*
Therapeutic Prog.	.00	.02*	-.00	-.09*
Prep. for Release	-.00	.03*	-.01	-.11*
	.00	.02*	.01	-.09*
Negative Conditions				
Resident Danger	.00	.00	.00	.20*
Danger from Staff	.00	-.00	-.00	.17*
Environ. Danger	.00	-.02*	-.01	.07*
Risks to Residents	-.00	-.02*	-.00	.10*
Freedom	.01*	.01	-.00	-.04

Table 8: The Effects of Individual Level Juvenile Characteristics on Juvenile Perceptions of Conditions of Confinement (B), page 3

Conditions of Confinement (DV)	Alcohol abuse	Drug abuse	Offense		
			Property	Person	Drug
Positive Conditions					
Control	-.15*	.04	.06	.04	.04
Activity	-.05	-.01	.06	.03	.01
Care	-.02	-.03	.04	-.01	-.02
Quality of Life	-.11*	-.06	.06*	.06	.05
Structure	.00	-.03	.06*	.05	.04
Justice	-.02	.00	.06	.02	-.01
Therapeutic Prog.	.01	-.02	.12*	.05	.06
Prep. for Release	.00	.03	-.00	-.01	.04
Negative Conditions					
Resident Danger	.02	.00	.01	-.00	-.01
Danger from Staff	.01	.05	.01	.04	.01
Environ. Danger	.12	-.09	-.08	-.05	.00
Risks to Residents	.22*	.01	-.06	-.04	-.03
Freedom	-.01	.01	-.03	-.04	-.02

Table 9: Staff Perceptions of Conditions of Confinement (means)

Condition of Confinement	Private Facilities			Public Facilities		
	M	SD	N	M	SD	N
Positive Conditions						
Control	4.09	.50	443	3.93	.53	884
Activity	4.42	.58	442	4.19	.59	883
Care	3.97	.52	444	3.79	.49	882
Quality of Life	3.77	.51	441	3.69	.54	877
Structure	4.26	.55	444	4.21	.51	883
Justice	4.21	.50	437	4.13	.49	867
Therapeutic Programs	3.87	.59	442	3.74	.61	876
Preparation for Release	4.34	.60	441	4.08	.78	876
Negative Conditions						
Resident Danger	2.16	.55	445	2.45	.57	886
Danger from Staff	2.25	.61	446	2.37	.68	886
Environmental Danger	1.85	.64	443	2.14	.61	886
Risks to Residents	1.75	.53	446	1.88	.57	886
Freedom	2.28	.59	441	2.38	.60	876

Note: Mean difference tested using t-test. $P > .05$

Table 10: The Effects of Operating Sector and Individual Level Covariates on Staff Perceptions of Conditions of Confinement (B)

Condition of Confinement	Operating Sector	p
Positive Conditions		
Control	.125	.25
Activity	.299*	.01
Care	.204*	.03
Quality of Life	.040	.64
Structure	.096	.28
Justice	.071	.36
Therapeutic Programs	.218*	.05
Preparation for Release	.293*	.03
Negative Conditions		
Resident Danger	-.142	.26
Danger from Staff	-.112	.42
Environmental Danger	-.221	.11
Risks to Residents	-.140	.14
Freedom	-.262*	.04

* p <.05

Table 11: The Effects of Facility Level Characteristics on Staff Perceptions of Conditions of Confinement (B), page 1

Condition of Confinement (DV) Confinement (DV)	Operating sector	Admission process index	Serious	Follow up data	Age
Positive Conditions					
Control	-.14	.14	-.07	.21*	-.0003
Activity	.03	.07	-.25*	.28*	-.0003
Care	.04	-.01	-.11	.22*	.0004
Quality of Life	-.17	.11	.04	.19*	-.0033
Structure	-.07	-.00	-.15	.27*	-.0015
Justice	-.08	.08	.07	.11	-.0006
Ther. Programs	.05	-.05	-.15	.27*	.0015
Prep. for Release	.16	-.25	-.06	.19	.0016
Negative Conditions					
Resident Danger	.07	-.12	.13	-.25	-.0006
Danger from Staff	.15	-.22	.22	-.38*	-.0017
Environ. Danger	.01	-.30	.22	-.34*	-.0019
Risks to Residents	.05	-.05	.10	-.28*	-.0010
Freedom	.11	-.09	.18	-.10	.00003

$p<.05$

Table 11: The Effects of Facility Level Characteristics on Staff Perceptions of Conditions of Confinement (B), page 2

Condition of Confinement (DV) Confinement (DV)	Capacity	Juvenile-staff ratio	No. of visiting hours
Positive Conditions			
Control	-.0003	.003	-.01
Activity	-.0012*	-.003	-.02
Care	-.0012*	-.005	-.01
Quality of Life	-.0010*	-.01	-.01
Structure	-.0004	-.01	-.01
Justice	-.0008*	-.003	-.01
Ther. Programs	-.0010*	-.01	-.01
Prep. for Release	-.0017*	.004	-.02
Negative Conditions			
Resident Danger	.0009	-.001	.01
Danger from Staff	.0010	.01	.01
Environ. Danger	.0010*	.01	.01
Risks to Residents	.0011*	.01	-.001
Freedom	-.0002	-.02	.01

Table 11: The Effects of Facility Level Characteristics on Staff Perceptions of Conditions of Confinement (B), page 3

Condition of Confinement (DV) Confinement (DV)	Type of Program			Region		
	Boot camp	Detention center	Training school	N	E	M
Positive Conditions						
Control	.19	-.30	-.11	-.03	.03	.06
Activity	-.10	-.65*	-.10	.22	.12	.12
Care	-.03	-.52*	-.06	.21	.18	.08
Quality of Life	-.21	-.49*	-.20	.15	.22*	.10
Structure	.08	-.33*	-.07	.11	.17*	.04
Justice	.02	-.23	-.13	.09	.03	.11
Ther. Programs	.09	-.56*	-.14	.10	.08	-.05
Prep. for Release	-.14	-.78*	-.22	.25	.09	.09
Negative Conditions						
Resident Danger	-.21	.38	.16	-.14	-.11	-.17
Danger from Staff	-.15	.44	.20	-.12	-.03	-.03
Environ. Danger	-.08	.20*	.15	-.26	-.28*	-.18
Risks to Residents	-.14	.26	.07	-.13	-.06	-.02
Freedom	-.44*	.06	-.06	.15	.18	.07

Table 12: The Effects of Individual Level Staff Characteristics on Staff Perceptions of Conditions of Confinement (B), page 1

Condition of Confinement (DV) Confinement (DV)	gender	age	race	prior years experience
Positive Conditions				
Control	.06*	.003	.01	-.007
Activity	.049	-.006*	.002	-.002
Care	.115*	.004*	.05	-.0006
Quality of Life	-.018	.005*	.033	-.004
Structure	.064*	.007*	.075*	-.009*
Justice	.041	.01	.021	-.001
Therap. Programs	.063	.004	.029	.005
Prep. for Release	.151*	.003	.049	.0002
Negative Conditions				
Resident Danger	-.018	-.003*	-.007	.003
Danger from Staff	.005	-.007*	.005	.001
Environ. Danger	.012	-.006*	.030	.011*
Risks to Residents	-.023	-.007*	.009	.003
Freedom	-.001	-.001	.01	.004

$p < .05$

Table 12: The Effects of Individual Level Staff Characteristics on Staff Perceptions of Conditions of Confinement (B), page 2

Condition of Confinement (DV)	Length of employment	Education Level		
		grad school	some college	high school
Positive Conditions				
Control	-.009*	.04	.04	.03
Activity	.0003	-.126*	.031	-.0003
Care	.0002	-.054	.041	.003
Quality of Life	-.005	-.016	.092*	.124*
Structure	-.004	-.070	.043	.073
Justice	-.005	-.106*	.098*	.135*
Therap. Programs	.004	-.008	.072	-.027
Prep. for Release	.007	-.021	.120*	.037
Negative Conditions				
Resident Danger	.011*	.002	-.026	.011
Danger from Staff	.018*	-.033	.0002	.038
Environ. Danger	.014*	-.021	-.053	-.082
Risks to Residents	.009*	.041	-.072	-.109*
Freedom	.007*	.018	-.037	-.081

$p < .05$

Table 13: Adjustment of Juveniles (means)

Time 1 Adjustment Outcomes	Private			Public		
	M	SD	N	M	SD	N
Social Attitudes	1.62	.14	180	1.61	.15	339
Depression*	3.11	.99	181	3.26	.97	342
Anxiety	1.41	.32	178	1.47	.33	340
Dysfunctional Impulsivity*	1.61	.36	178	1.67	.33	342
Social Bonds*	3.67	.61	182	3.48	.67	348

Time 2 Adjustment Outcomes	Private			Public		
	M	SD	N	M	SD	N
Social Attitudes*	1.63	.16	170	1.59	.16	328
Depression*	2.94	1.1	177	3.05	1.0	337
Anxiety	1.41	.30	175	1.40	.31	334
Dysfunctional Impulsivity*	1.59	.36	172	1.65	.33	332
Social Bonds*	3.52	.66	182	3.49	.66	348

$p < .05$

Note: Mean difference tested using a nested analysis-of-variance, with facilities nested within operating sector.

Table 14: Change in Juvenile Outcome Measures between Survey Administration

Dependent Variable Change Score	Private			Public		
	M	SD	N	M	SD	N
Social Attitudes*	.012	.16	170	-.012	.15	328
Anxiety	.008	.32	175	-.065	.35	334
Dysfunctional Impulsivity*	-.189	.36	172	-.015	.37	332
Depression	-.166	1.24	177	-.209	1.0	337
Social Bonds	-.169	.65	182	.005	.60	348

Note: Mean difference are tested using a nested analysis-of-variance, with facilities nested within operating sector. $p < .05$

Table 15: The Effect of Operating Sector and Individual Covariates on the Adjustment of Juveniles (B)

Covariates	Pro-Social Attitudes	Dysfunctional Impulsivity	Anxiety	Social Bonds
Intercept	-.008	-.029	-.040	-.051
OPERATING SECTOR	.026	.014	.093	-.216*
Age	-.011	.017	.038*	-.008
Gender	-.021	-.014	.143	-.119
Race	.017	-.032	-.041	.129
Alcohol abuse	-.043	-.100	-.060	-.143
Drug abuse	.023	.116	.024	.127
Child abuse and family Violence	.003	-.026	-.065*	.022
Sentence length	-.001	-.001	.002	-.003
Time in facility	.004*	.008*	.002	-.007
Age at 1st arrest	-.004	.009	-.018	-.012
No. of previous commitments	.003	.009	-.002	.039*
Property offense	-.022	-.000	-.015	.104
Person offense	-.016	-.012	-.056	.112
Drug offense	-.022	-.005	-.067	.267*

*p<.05

Note: Variables in upper case indicate level-2 variables.

Table 16: The Effect of Operating Sector, Facility and Individual Covariates on the Adjustment of Juveniles (B)

Covariates	Pro-Social Attitudes	Dysfunctional Impulsivity	Anxiety	Social Bonds
Intercept	-.009	-.038	-.044	-.039
OPERATING SECTOR	-.013	.068	.146*	-.294*
AGE	-.000	.001	.002	-.004
ADMISSION PROCESS	.129	-.345	.041	.323
CAPACITY	-.000	.000	-.000	.000
SERIOUSNESS	.001	.014	-.080	.095
BOOT CAMP	.009	.042	.011	-.076
DETENTION CENTER	-.049	.199	-.084	-.045
TRAINING SCHOOL	-.022	-.023	.037	.146
JUVENILE-STAFF RATIO	-.002	.012	-.005	-.001
VISITING HOURS	-.001	.005	.014	-.016
FOLLOW UP DATA	.010	-.018	.081	-.203
NORTH REGION	.054	-.190	.059	.129
EAST REGION	.060	-.119	-.053	.125
MIDWEST REGION	.027	-.039	-.028	.104
WEST REGION	-.077	.124	.152	-.322
PERC'D ENVIRONMENT	.020	.114	-.002	-.056
Age	-.012	.018	.042*	-.017
Gender	.011	-.104	.132	-.027
Race	.016	-.030	-.052	.131
Alcohol abuse	-.045	-.090	-.055	-.175
Drug abuse	.022	.108	.035	.137
Child abuse /family violence	.001	-.022	-.070*	.024
Sentence	-.001	-.001	.003	-.004
Time in facility	.004*	.009*	.001	-.008
Age at 1st arrest	-.006	.011	-.021*	-.007
No. of previous commitments	.005	.006	-.004	.044*
Property offense	-.025	.001	-.017	.102
Person offense	-.009	-.022	-.064	.127
Drug offense	-.034	.014	-.055	.234*

Note: Variables in upper case indicate level-2 variables. $p<.05$

Table 17: Staff Work Experiences (means)

Work Experiences	Private			Public		
	M	SD	N	M	SD	N
Staff Communication*	3.68	.79	413	3.52	.76	803
Stress*	1.97	.63	427	2.02	.67	832
Job Satisfaction*	3.64	.57	426	3.52	.55	833
Staff Support*	3.69	.71	430	3.54	.68	834

Note: Mean difference are tested using a nested analysis-of-variance, with facilities nested within operating sector. $p < .05$

Table 18: The Effects of Operating Sector and Individual Level Covariates on Staff Work Experiences (B)

Covariates	Staff Communication	Stress	Job Satisfaction	Staff Support
Intercept	3.59*	2.00*	3.57*	3.59*
OPERATING SECTOR	.134	-.035	.0136	.126
age	.008*	-.008*	.005*	.007*
length of employment	-.014*	.017*	-.008*	-.015*
yrs of prior experience	-.008	.0001	-.008	-.006
gender	-.037	.189*	-.032	-.023
race (white/nonwhite)	.197*	-.172*	.132*	.186*
high school	.141	-.015	.105	.129
some college	.178*	.016	.119*	.128*
grad school	-.026	.024	-.063	-.052

* $p<.05$

Note: Variables in upper case indicate level-2 variables.

Table 19: The Effect of Operating Sector, Facility and Individual Covariates on Staff Work Experience (B)

Covariates	Staff Communication	Stress	Job Satisfaction	Staff Support
Intercept	3.58*	2.00*	3.55*	3.57*
OPERATING SECTOR	.106	.018	.092	.103
AGE	.001	-.001	.001	.000
ADMISSION PROCESS	-.027	-.294*	-.088	-.239
CAPACITY	-.000	.000	-.000	-.000
SERIOUSNESS	-.027	-.081	-.041	.007
BOOT CAMP	.015	-.026	-.070	-.065
DETENTION CENTER	.145	.040	.125	.122
TRAINING SCHOOL	.055	.060	-.072	.002
JUVENILE-STAFF ratio	-.003	.019*	-.003	.002
VISITING HOURS	.006	-.001	.013	.005
FOLLOW UP DATA	.190	-.143	.087	.087
NORTH REGION	-.010	.067	-.023	.104
EAST REGION	.095	.032	-.061	.006
MIDWEST REGION	.025	.079	.047	-.006
WEST REGION	.267	-.111	.203	.332*
PERC'D ENVIRONMENT	.267*	-.108	.310*	.377*
age	.007*	-.009*	.005*	.007*
length of employment	-.012*	.013*	-.007	-.014*
yrs of prior experience	-.008	.000	-.007	-.006
gender	-.016	.173*	-.013	-.001
race (white/nonwhite)	.222*	-.197*	.157*	.210*
high school	.150	-.007	.118	.140*
some college	.174*	.028	.125*	.131*
grad school	-.009	.003	-.047	-.033

Note: Variables in upper case indicate level-2 variables. $p<.05$

Figure 1: Impact of Operating Sector and Conditions on Juvenile Adjustment and Staff Experiences.

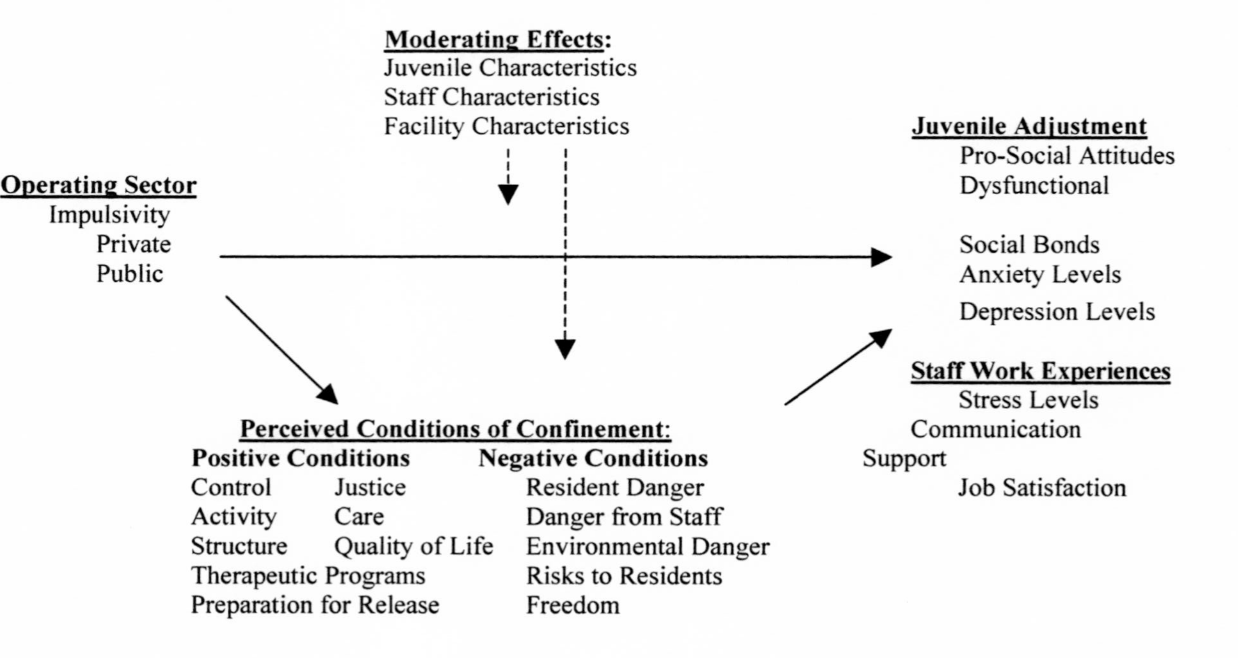

Figure 2: The Indirect Effect of Operating Sector on Conditions of Confinement

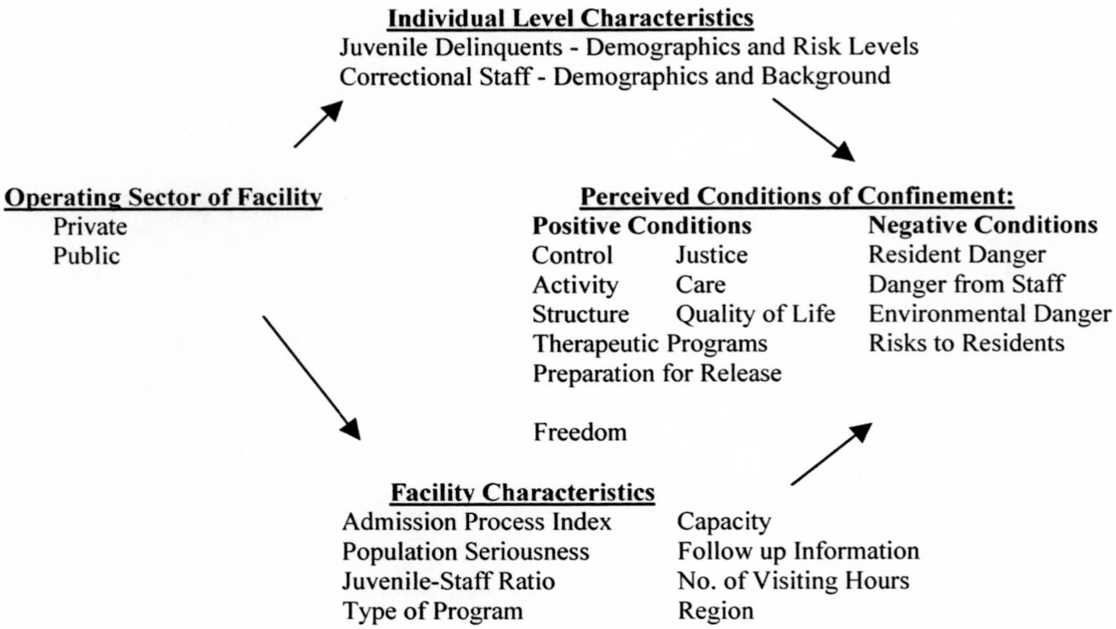

Appendix A: Juvenile Conditions of Confinement Scales

1. Juvenile Control Scale Items	Mean	SD	Item to Total Correlation
Staff members ignore conflicts among residents.	2.25	1.3	.525
Residents do what the staff here tell them to do.	3.67	1.2	.497
Nothing will anything happen to a resident if they break a rule.	2.39	1.5	.435
Residents criticize staff members without getting in trouble for it.	2.35	1.4	.545
If residents argue with each other, they will get into trouble.	3.48	1.4	.480
Staff members check up on the residents regularly.	3.93	1.3	.496
Residents can get weapons at this facility.	2.27	1.5	.659
Residents can escape from this facility.	2.78	1.5	.524
Visitors can bring drugs into this facility for residents.	2.12	1.5	.639

Scale Mean (SD): Public: 3.62 (.75) Private: 3.74 (.75)
Range: 1-5
Cronbach's alpha: .695
N: Public: 2629 Private: 1159

2. Juvenile Resident Danger Scale Items	Mean	SD	Item to Total Correlation
I am concerned with being hit or punched by other residents.	1.97	1.4	.621
I am afraid of other residents at this institution.	1.50	1.1	.539
Residents say mean things to other residents at this institution.	3.40	1.4	.577
Residents use weapons when they fight.	1.68	1.1	.650
Residents fight with other residents here.	2.77	1.5	.739
Residents are sexually attached in this institution.	1.49	1.0	.568
Residents are extremely dangerous here.	2.03	1.2	.727
Residents have to defend themselves against other residents in this institution.	2.64	1.5	.754

Scale Mean (SD): Public: 2.27 (.81) Private: 2.00 (.83)
Range: 1-5
Cronbach's alpha : .801
N: Public: 2628 Private: 1152

3. Juvenile Danger from Staff Scale Items	Mean	SD	Item to Total Correlation
Residents fear staff at this institution.	2.31	1.4	.651
Staff say mean things to residents.	3.00	1.4	.732
Residents are in danger of being hit or punched by staff here.	2.12	1.4	.819
Residents say they have been hurt by staff here.	2.29	1.4	.776
Staff grab, push or shove residents at this institution.	2.79	1.5	.764
I am afraid of staff at this institution.	1.89	1.4	.687

Scale Mean (SD): Public: 2.38 (1.0) Private: 2.46 (1.1)
Range: 1-5
Cronbach's alpha: .830
N: Public: 2607 Private: 1143

4. Juvenile Environmental Danger Items	Mean	SD	Item to Total Correlation
If a resident believes he will be hurt by another resident, the staff will protect him.	3.40	1.5	.651
My property is safe here.	3.00	1.6	.613
There are gangs here.	2.81	1.7	.494
It is safer for residents who ARE members of a gang.	2.25	1.5	.427
Staff have caught and punished the real trouble makers among residents.	3.17	1.3	.553
There are enough staff to keep residents safe here.	3.36	1.5	.692
Staff prevent violence among residents.	3.36	1.5	.687
Staff prevent forced sex among residents.	3.53	1.7	.567

Scale Mean (SD): Public: 2.80 (.94) Private: 2.51 (.98)
Range: 1-5
Cronbach's alpha: .729
N: Public: 2578 Private: 1141

5. Juvenile Activity Scale Items	Mean	SD	Item to Total Correlation
A counselor is available for me to talk to if I need one.	3.67	1.3	.673
I have things to do that keep me busy here.	3.81	1.3	.758
I spend time on school work.	3.47	1.4	.657
I can find something to do here at night.	3.27	1.5	.618
I am encouraged to plan for what I will be doing when I leave here.	4.02	1.3	.647
I get exercise here.	4.36	1.1	.596
There are things to do here when I am not in school.	3.95	1.3	.738

Scale Mean (SD): Public: 3.20 (.71) Private: 3.37 (.79)
Range: 1-5
Cronbach's alpha: .792
N: Public: 2575 Private: 1142

6. Juvenile Care Scale Items	Mean	SD	Item to Total Correlation
The staff encourage me to try new activities.	3.42	1.4	.569
Additional help with school work outside of classroom hours is available to me.	2.95	1.5	.613
Staff tease depressed residents.	2.60	1.4	.568
Residents give other residents with personal problem a hard time.	2.91	1.3	.520
The health care here is good.	3.33	1.4	.579
Other residents are unfriendly.	3.00	1.2	.450
No one will help me if I have a problem.	2.52	1.3	.469
Staff care about residents here.	3.31	1.4	.665
Staff and residents don't respect each other here.	2.69	1.4	.411
Residents who have been here longer help new residents when they arrive.	3.27	1.4	.979

Scale Mean (SD): Public: 3.20 (.71) Private: 3.37 (.79)
Range: 1-5
Cronbach's alpha: .728
N: Public: 2568 Private: 1140

7. Juvenile Risk to Residents Scale Items	Mean	SD	Item to Total Correlation
Insects, rodents and dirt are a problem here.	2.72	1.5	.679
There is a bad odor or poor air circulation.	3.64	1.5	.709
Residents know what to do in case of a fire.	3.98	1.4	.459
There are things lying around that could help a fire spread.	2.49	1.5	.620
People could get hurt because the place is so dirty.	2.09	1.4	.759
Many accidents happen here.	2.38	1.3	.707
Most of the jobs we have to do are safe.	3.69	1.3	.509

Scale Mean (SD): Public: 2.47 (.87) Private: 2.40 (.85)
Range: 1-5
Cronbach's alpha: .757
N: Public: 2575 Private: 1151

8. Juvenile Quality of Life Scale Items	Mean	SD	Item to Total Correlation
I get exercise here.	4.36	1.1	.294
One thing bad about this place is that it's so noisy.	2.96	1.4	.455
My living area here has a lot of space.	2.54	1.4	.517
I have privacy here in the shower/toilet area.	2.34	1.6	.485
The food here is good.	2.77	1.4	.581
I get enough to eat here.	2.97	1.5	.614
The visiting areas are crowded here.	2.68	1.4	.461
It is hard to talk with visitors because the noise is too loud here.	2.38	1.4	.482
I can read and/or study without being bothered here.	2.78	1.4	.596
I can be alone when I want to here.	1.89	1.3	.405

Scale Mean (SD): Public: 2.95 (.67) Private: 2.97 (.70)
Range: 1-5
Cronbach's alpha: .665
N: Public: 2552 Private: 1139

9. Juvenile Structure Scale Items	Mean	SD	Item to Total Correlation
I have a set schedule to follow each day here.	4.20	1.3	.509
I am required to study at certain times here.	3.47	1.5	.527
I know what will happen if I break a rule here.	4.27	1.1	.574
My living area looks messy here.	1.86	1.2	.528
Many residents look messy here.	2.43	1.3	.569
Staff are always changing their minds about the rules here.	2.98	1.4	.544
Different staff members here have different rules so you never know what you are supposed to do.	3.28	1.4	.469
I know when I can take a shower here.	4.08	1.3	.518
I know when the recreation facilities are available for me to use here.	3.40	1.6	.474
Staff here let me know what is expected of me.	4.04	1.2	.610

Scale Mean (SD): Public: 3.67 (.71) Private: 3.73 (.73)
Range: 1-5
Cronbach's alpha: .720
N: Public: 2541 Private: 1136

10. Juvenile Justice Scale Items	Mean	SD	Item to Total Correlation
Residents are punished even when they don't do anything wrong.	3.19	1.4	.590
Staff use force when they don't really need to.	2.87	1.4	.643
I can file a grievance (formal complaint) against staff members.	3.66	1.5	.474
I am aware of the grievance process.	3.65	1.5	.461
Problems between staff and residents can be worked out easily.	3.14	1.3	.628
It doesn't do any good to file a grievance against staff members.	3.18	1.5	.295
Something bad might happen to me if I file a grievance.	2.49	1.4	.569
I usually deserve any punishment that I receive.	2.91	1.3	.526
Punishments given are fair.	2.82	1.3	.656
Staff treat residents fairly.	3.02	1.3	.717
I can talk to my lawyer when I want.	2.35	1.5	.512

Scale Mean (SD): Public: 3.05 (.75) Private: 3.13 (.82)
Range: 1-5
Cronbach's alpha : .769
N: Public: 2530 Private: 1135

11. Juvenile Freedom Scale Items	Mean	SD	Item to Total Correlation
I have to work even if I do not want to.	3.96	1.3	.429
Residents choose the type of work they do here.	2.22	1.4	.614
I can read whenever I want.	2.74	1.5	.632
I can listen to music when I want.	1.63	1.1	.624
Residents have a say about what goes on here.	2.29	1.4	.588
I can go where I want when I want to in this facility.	1.52	1.0	.525
Residents are encouraged to make their own decisions.	2.87	1.5	.532

Scale Mean (SD): Public: 2.34 (.78) Private: 2.09 (.72)
Range: 1-5
Cronbach's alpha: .640
N: Public: 2535 Private: 1132

12. Therapeutic Programs Scale Items	Mean	SD	Item to Total Correlation
My experiences will help me find a job when I get out.	3.51	1.4	.758
The things I do here help keep me focused on my goals for the future.	3.69	1.3	.795
Being here helps me understand myself.	3.51	1.4	.786
I learn things in educational courses given here.	3.75	1.3	.748
By trying new activities I am learning skills I can use when I leave.	3.79	1.3	.786
Things I learn here will help me with future school work.	3.72	1.3	.789
Substance abuse treatment services here help many residents.	3.18	1.4	.681
The opportunities for religious services here help me become a better person.	3.30	1.4	.622
I feel healthier since coming here.	3.43	1.5	.621
The individual attention here has helped me.	2.98	1.5	.704

Scale Mean (SD): Public: 3.46 (1.0) Private: 3.55 (.99)
Range: 1-5
Cronbach's alpha: .900
N: Public: 2529 Private: 1131

13. Juvenile Preparation for Release Scale Items	Mean	SD	Item to Total Correlation
I have made plans to find a job or have already found a place to work when I leave here.	4.31	1.4	.422
I have set goals for myself.	4.72	.97	.428
I have planned a place to live when I leave here.	4.55	1.2	.380
I have had a chance to get organized with the school I plan to attend when I leave here.	3.29	1.9	.402
I have had a chance to meet with my future probation officer.	2.85	1.9	.329
If I need drug or alcohol treatment, I have had a chance to make plans for future treatment.	3.51	1.8	.455
I am encouraged to plan for what I will be doing when I leave here.	4.07	1.2	.631

Scale Mean (SD): Public: 3.80 (.72) Private: 3.89 (.70)
Range: 1-5
Cronbach's alpha: .448
N: Public: 2738 Private: 1180

Appendix B: Juvenile Risk Scales

1. Juvenile Alcohol Abuse Scale Items	Mean	SD	Item to Total Correlation
Have you ever gone to school while you were under the influence of alcohol?	1.52	.50	.688
Have you ever stolen money from friends or family to buy alcohol without them knowing?	1.77	.42	.632
Have you ever received treatment for alcohol abuse?	1.74	.44	.622
In the six months before you entered a juvenile facility, did you drink heavily, get drunk often, or have a drinking problem?	1.61	.49	.742
Has anyone including someone at school ever talked to you because they were concerned that you may have a problem with alcohol?	1.74	.44	.671

Scale Mean (SD): Public: 1.31 (.31) Private: 1.34 (.31)
Range: 1-2
Cronbach's alpha: .695
N: Public: 2712 Private: 1167

2. Juvenile Drug Abuse Scale Items	Mean	SD	Item to Total Correlation
Have you ever gone to school high on drugs?	1.34	.47	.626
Have you ever stolen money from friends or family to buy drugs without them knowing?	1.69	.46	.735
Has anyone including someone at school ever talked to you because they were concerned that you may have a problem with drugs?	1.62	.49	.599
Have you ever received treatment for drug abuse?	1.68	.46	.505
In the six months before you entered a juvenile facility, did you use a lot of drugs, get high often, or have a drug problem?	1.42	.49	.652

Scale Mean (SD): Public: 1.44(.33) Private: 1.47(.33)
Range: 1-2
Cronbach's alpha: .544
N: Public: 2743 Private: 1184

3. Juvenile Family Violence/Child Abuse Items	Mean	SD	Item to Total Correlation
How often did your mother or father slap you?	2.06	1.1	.739
How often did your mother or father hit you?	2.09	1.2	.766
How often were you burned by your mother or father?	1.12	.56	.529
How often did you have bruises, cuts, or other evidence of punishment by your mother or father?	1.50	.97	.813
How often were you scared or afraid of getting physically hurt by your mother or father?	1.62	1.1	.775
Would you say that you were unfed, unwashed, or generally unsupervised at home on some regular basis as a young child?	1.34	.89	.601
How often did you witness one parent physically harm the other parent?	1.65	1.0	.682
How often did you witness a member of your family physically harm another family member?	1.76	1.1	.678
How often were you touched in a sexual way or forced to have sex by an adult or older child when you did not want this to happen?	1.21	.72	.506

Scale Mean (SD): Public: 1.61 (.70) Private: 1.56 (.63)
Range: 1-5
Cronbach's alpha: .854

N: Public: 2726 Private: 1181

Appendix C: Juvenile Adjustment and Change Scales

1. Juvenile Risk Taking Behavior Scale Items	Mean	SD	Item to Total Correlation
I like to take chances.	1.23	.42	.582
I like to do things that are exciting or strange.	1.24	.43	.626
I only do things that feel safe.	1.65	.48	.725
I am very careful and cautious.	1.44	.50	.641

Scale Mean (SD): Public: 1.66 (.30) Private: 1.66(.30)
Range: 1-2
Cronbach's alpha: .560
N: Public: 2665 Private: 1158

2. Juvenile Dysfunctional Impulsivity Scale Items	Mean	SD	Item to Total Correlation
I will say whatever comes into my head without thinking first.	1.55	.52	.686
I don't spend enough time thinking over a situation before I act.	1.39	.49	.682
I get into trouble because I don't think before I act.	1.29	.46	.716
I say and do thinks without considering the consequences.	1.33	.47	.739

Scale Mean (SD): Public: 1.61(.34) Private: 1.62 (.34)
Range: 1-2
Cronbach's alpha: .659
N: Public: 2672 Private: 1160

3. Juvenile Social Bonds Scale Items	Mean	SD	Item to Total Correlation
I would like to be like my parents.	3.21	1.4	.500
I feel comfortable talking to my parents if I have a problem.	3.38	1.4	.502
I feel bad when I do something my parents wouldn't like.	3.57	1.3	.616
I can count on my parents to stick by me.	4.33	1.2	.434
I want my children to respect me.	4.78	.71	.360
It is important for people to spend time with their families.	4.58	.87	.521
I like school.	3.20	1.2	.615
Finishing my homework is important to me.	2.96	1.3	.670
I respect my teachers.	3.54	1.3	.622
Getting good grades is important.	3.78	1.3	.673
I don't care what my teachers think of me.	2.78	1.5	.301
It would make me feel bad if my teachers criticized me.	2.38	1.5	.433
I get into trouble at school like being suspended or expelled.	3.15	1.3	.374
A good education is important to me.	4.39	1.1	.587
The most important things that happen to me involve my job.	2.31	1.4	.365
I enjoy thinking about where I will work in the future.	3.86	1.3	.595
Doing well at work is important to me.	3.98	1.3	.606
I feel good when I do my job well.	4.35	1.2	.581

Scale Mean (SD): Public: 3.60 (.69) Private: 3.64 (.63) Range: 1-5

Cronbach's alpha: .836 N: Public: 2775 Private: 1193

4. Juvenile Pro-Social Attitudes Scale Items	Mean	SD	Item to Total Correlation
I worry too much about doing the right things.	1.51	.50	.116
I am smarter than most people I know.	1.37	.48	.112
A person never knows when he will get mad, or have trouble.	1.34	.47	.282
A person is better off if he doesn't trust people.	1.58	.49	.390
Most police are pretty dumb.	1.49	.50	.448
A person like me fights first and asks questions later.	1.56	.50	.487
If I could, I'd just as soon quit school or my job right now.	1.83	.37	.335
I don't care if people like me or not.	1.35	.48	.321
I have a real mean streak in me.	1.47	.50	.493
Most of the time I can't seem to find anything to do.	1.52	.50	.379
It's fun to give the police a bad time.	1.54	.50	.479
I really don't have very man problems to worry about.	1.62	.49	.116
If a bunch of you are in trouble, you should stick together on a story.	1.24	.46	.337
I have a lot of headaches.	1.69	.46	.331
I would usually prefer to be alone than with others.	1.56	.50	.263
I would never back down from a fight.	1.44	.50	.413
I have a lot of bad things on my mind that people don't know about.	1.33	.47	.479
Parents are always nagging and picking on young people.	1.75	.43	.368
At night when I have nothing to do I like to go out and find a little excitement.	1.24	.43	.375
A lot of women seem bossy and mean.	1.64	.48	.353
I am always kind.	1.58	.49	.176

I worry most of the time.	1.53	.50	.346
If you're not in with the right people, you may be in for some real trouble.	1.28	.45	.201
My mind is full of bad thoughts.	1.68	.50	.500
Sometimes when my family tells me not to do something, I do it anyway.	1.20	.40	.502
I hardly ever feel excited or thrilled.	1.71	.45	.315
The people who run things are usually against me.	1.68	.47	.418
I like to read and study.	1.41	.49	.251
I often have trouble getting my breath.	1.75	.43	.286
For my size, I'm really pretty tough.	1.21	.41	.203
People hardly ever give me a fair chance.	1.62	.49	.436
Sometimes the only way to really settle something is to fight it out.	1.48	.50	.473
I am nervous.	1.69	.46	.315
Stealing isn't so bad if it's from a rich person.	1.74	.44	.416
I feel better when I know exactly what will happen from one day to the next.	1.24	.43	.203

Scale Mean (SD): Public: 1.50 (.14) Private: 1.51 (.13)
Range: 1-2
Cronbach's alpha: .771

N: Public: 2649 Private: 1161

5. Juvenile Depression Scale Items	Mean	SD	Item to Total Correlation
At times I worry too much about things that don't really matter.	2.75	1.3	.609
Sometimes, recently, I have worried about losing my mind.	3.30	1.5	.740
I often feel angry these days.	2.58	1.3	.735
In the past few weeks, I have felt depressed and very unhappy.	2.69	1.4	.741
These days I can't help wondering if anything is worthwhile any more.	3.27	1.4	.755

Scale Mean (SD): Public: 3.11 (1.0) Private: 3.01 (.98)
Range: 1-5
Cronbach's alpha: .763
N: Public: 2710 Private: 1174

6. Juvenile Anxiety Scale Items	Mean	SD	Item to Total Correlation
I feel calm.	1.28	.45	.581
I feel upset.	1.61	.49	.686
I feel anxious.	1.44	.50	.478
I feel nervous.	1.64	.48	.683
I am relaxed.	1.38	.51	.669
I am worried.	1.49	.50	.683

Scale Mean (SD): Public: 1.42 (.31) Private: 1.40 (.30)
Range: 1-2
Cronbach's alpha: .705
N: Public: 2689 Private: 1169

Appendix D: Staff Conditions of Confinement Scales

1. Activity	Mean	SD	Item to Total Correlation
A counselor is available for the residents to talk to if they need one.	4.26	.89	.589
Residents have things to do that keep them busy here.	4.22	.84	.797
Residents spend time on school work.	3.93	.90	.700
Residents can find something to do here at night.	3.92	1.1	.649
Residents are encouraged to plan for what they will be doing when they leave here.	4.50	.75	.677
Residents get exercise here.	4.64	.66	.667
There are things for residents to do here when they are not in school.	4.36	.85	.783

Scale mean (SD): Private: 4.42(.58) Public: 4.19(.59)
Range: 1-5
Cronbach's alpha: .754
N: Private: 883 Public: 442

2. Freedom	Mean	SD	Item to Total Correlation
Residents have to work even if they do not want to.	3.77	1.2	.551
Residents choose the type of work they do here.	2.37	1.0	.703
Residents can read whenever they want.	2.64	1.1	.627
Residents can listen to music when they want.	1.83	.95	.654
Residents have a say about what goes on here.	2.38	1.1	.674
Residents can go where they want whenever they want to in this facility.	1.33	.71	.408
Residents are encouraged to make their own decisions.	3.72	1.1	.428

Scale mean (SD): Private: 2.28(.59) Public: 2.38(.60)
Range: 1-5
Cronbach's alpha: .683
N: Private: 876 Public: 441

3. Therapeutic Programming	Mean	SD	Item to Total Correlation
Residents' experiences here will help them find a job when they get out.	3.38	.86	.669
The things residents do here help to keep them focused on their goals for the future.	3.83	.85	.791
Being here helps residents understand themselves.	3.73	.81	.780
Residents learn things in the educational courses given here.	4.07	.80	.768
By trying new activities residents are learning skills they can use when they leave.	3.95	.86	.784
Things residents learn here will help them with future school work.	4.01	.81	.798
The substance abuse treatment services here help many residents.	3.49	.95	.667
The opportunities for religious services here help residents to become better people.	3.49	.92	.593
The individual attention here has helped residents.	3.80	.78	.734
Residents are healthier since they have come here.	4.09	.77	.579

Scale mean (SD): Private: 3.87 (.59) Public: 3.74 (.61)
Range: 1-5
Cronbach's alpha: .893
N: Private: 876 Public: 442

4. Risk to Residents Scale	Mean	SD	Item to Total Correlation
Insects, rodents and dirt are a problem here.	2.03	1.0	.660
There is a bad odor or poor air circulation.	2.21	1.1	.688
Residents know what to do in case of a fire.	4.46	.87	.547
There are things lying around that could help a fire spread.	2.01	.98	.662
People could get hurt because the place is so dirty.	1.45	.73	.684
Many accidents happen here.	2.00	.66	.572
Most of the jobs residents have to do are safe.	4.35	.91	.506

Scale mean (SD): Private: 1.75(.53) Public: 1.88 (.57)
Range: 1-5
Cronbach's alpha: .734
N: Private: 886 Public:446

5. Justice	Mean	SD	Item to Total Correlation
Residents are punished even when they don't do anything wrong.	1.86	.81	.529
Staff use force when they don't really need to.	1.68	.74	.571
Residents can file a grievance (formal complaint) against staff members.	4.45	1.0	.523
Residents are aware of the grievance process.	4.44	.92	.583
Problems between staff and residents can be worked out easily.	3.74	.76	.483
It doesn't do any good for the residents to file a grievance against staff members.	2.20	1.1	.526
Something bad might happen to residents if they file a grievance.	1.40	.74	.570
Residents usually deserve the punishment that they receive.	4.05	.78	.517
Punishments given are fair.	4.20	.78	.652
Staff treat residents fairly.	4.25	.71	.675
Residents can talk to their lawyer when they want to.	3.70	1.3	.516

Scale mean (SD): Private: 4.21(.50) Public: 4.13 (.49)
Range: 1-5
Cronbach's alpha: .773
N: Private: 867 Public: 437

6. Structure Scale	Mean	SD	Item to Total Correlation
Residents have a set schedule to follow each day here.	4.72	.63	.529
Residents are required to study at certain times here.	4.05	1.1	.599
Residents know what will happen if they break a rule.	4.46	.75	.650
Residents' living area looks messy here.	1.88	.81	.608
Many residents look messy here.	1.98	.82	.637
Staff change their minds about the rules here.	2.31	.97	.675
Different staff have different rules so the residents never know what they are supposed to do.	2.34	1.0	.646
Residents know when they can take a shower here.	4.62	.72	.553
Residents know when the recreation facilities are available for them to use here.	4.33	1.0	.494
Staff here let residents know what is expected of them.	2.93	1.2	.710

Scale mean (SD): Private: 4.26 (.55) Public: 4.21 (.51)
Range: 1-5
Cronbach's alpha: .810
N: Private: 883 Public: 444

7. Care Scale	Mean	SD	Item to Total Correlation
The staff encourage residents to try new activities.	3.92	.88	.578
Additional help with school work outside of classroom hours is available to residents.	3.48	1.1	.640
Staff tease depressed residents.	1.62	.80	.631
Residents give other residents with personal problems a hard time.	2.63	.85	.513
The health care for the residents here is good.	4.19	.92	.614
Residents are unfriendly.	2.60	.69	.476
No one will help residents if they have a problem.	1.80	1.1	.509
Staff care about residents here.	4.35	.76	.646
Staff and residents don't respect each other here.	2.34	.93	.557
Residents who have been here longer help new residents when they arrive.	3.52	1.0	.426

Scale mean (SD): Private: 2.16 (.55) Public: 2.45 (.57)
Range: 1-5
Cronbach's alpha: .860
N: Private: 882 Public: 444

8. Resident Danger Scale	Mean	SD	Item to Total Correlation
Residents are concerned with being hit or punched by other residents.	2.64	.84	.760
Residents are afraid of other residents here.	2.62	.75	.729
Residents say mean things to other residents.	3.17	.85	.678
Residents use weapons when they fight.	1.59	.69	.664
Residents fight with other residents here.	2.64	.86	.767
Residents are sexually attacked in this institution.	1.53	.69	.669
Residents are extremely dangerous here.	2.34	.94	.644
Residents have to defend themselves against other residents in this institution.	2.30	.86	.786

Scale mean (SD): Private: 2.16 (.55) Public: 2.45 (.57)
Range: 1-5
Cronbach's alpha: .860
N: Private: 886 Public:445

9. Staff Danger Scale	Mean	SD	Item to Total Correlation
Residents say mean things to staff.	2.78	.86	.760
Staff are in danger of being hit or punched by residents here.	2.50	.88	.806
Residents, grab, push, or shove staff at this institution.	1.97	.76	.795
Staff are afraid of some residents at this institution.	2.06	.86	.760

Scale mean (SD): Private: 2.25(.61) Public: 2.37 (.68)
Range: 1-5
Cronbach's alpha: .784
N: Private: 886 Public: 446

10. Environmental Danger Scale	Mean	SD	Item to Total Correlation
If a resident believes he will be hurt by another resident, the staff will protect him.	4.38	.87	.591
Residents' property is safe here.	3.99	1.0	.637
There are gangs here.	2.61	1.5	.659
It is safer for residents who ARE members of a gang.	2.08	1.2	.521
Staff have caught and punished the real trouble makers among residents.	3.77	.89	.494
There are enough staff to keep other staff members safe here.	3.49	1.2	.632
Staff prevent violence among residents.	4.17	.77	.676
Staff prevent forced sex among residents.	4.49	.89	.554

Scale mean (SD): Private: 1.85(.64) Public: 2.14 (.61)
Range: 1-5
Cronbach's alpha: .742
N: Private: 886 Public: 443

11. Quality of Life	Mean	SD	Item to Total Correlation
Residents get exercise here.	4.64	.66	.389
One thing bad about this place is that it's so noisy.	2.42	.87	.493
Residents' living area here has a lot of space.	3.24	1.2	.535
Residents have privacy here in the shower /toilet area.	2.88	1.4	.469
The food residents eat here is good.	3.73	.97	.572
Residents get enough to eat here.	4.06	1.0	.581
The visiting areas are crowded here.	2.41	1.0	.564
It is hard for residents to talk with visitors because the noise is too loud here.	1.92	.86	.565

Scale mean (SD): Private: 3.77 (.57) Public: 3.69 (.54)
Range: 1-5
Cronbach's alpha: .629
N: Private: 877 Public: 441

12. Preparation for Release	Mean	SD	Item to Total Correlation
Residents are encouraged to plan for what they will be doing when they leave.	4.50	.75	.377
Residents have made plans to find a job or have already found a place to work when they leave here.	1.94	.89	.525
Residents have set goals for themselves.	1.31	.69	.548
Residents have planned a place to live when they leave here.	1.38	.72	.589
Residents have had a chance to get organized with the school they plan to attend when they leave here.	1.59	.85	.628
Residents have had a chance to meet with their future probation officers.	1.74	.90	.550
If residents need drug or alcohol treatment when they leave here they have had a chance to make plans for future treatment.	1.42	.79	.624

Scale mean (SD): Private: 4.34 (.60) Public: 4.08 (.78)
Range: 1-5
Cronbach's alpha: .650
N: Private: 876 Public: 441

13. Control Scale	Mean	SD	Item to Total Correlation
Residents do what the staff here tell them to do.	4.05	.66	.502
Nothing will happen to a resident if they break a rule.	2.56	1.2	.422
Staff members ignore conflicts among residents.	1.64	.81	.575
Residents criticize staff members without getting in trouble for it.	2.35	1.0	.639
If residents argue with each other, they will get into trouble.	3.67	.97	.640
Staff members check upon the residents regularly.	4.57	.74	.499
Residents can get weapons at this facility.	1.76	.95	.606
Residents can escape from this facility.	2.28	.97	.517
Visitors can bring drugs into facility for residents.	1.85	.95	.662

Scale mean (SD): Private: 4.09 (.50) Public: 3.93 (.53)
Range: 1-5
Cronbach's alpha: .723
N: Private: 884 Public: 443

14. Job Satisfaction Scale	Mean	SD	Item to Total Correlation
Training at this facility has improved my job skills.	3.54	1.0	.639
The training program here does not prepare me to deal with situations that arise.	3.63	1.0	.677
Information I get by formal communication channels helps me perform my job well.	2.39	1.0	.447
In this facility, it's unclear who has the formal authority to make a decision.	2.21	1.1	.638
I am told promptly when there's a change in policy, rules, or regulations that affect me.	3.58	1.1	.653
It's really not possible to change how things run here.	2.85	1.1	.382
I have the authority I need to accomplish my work objectives.	3.78	.97	.671
Management at this facility is flexible enough to make changes when necessary.	3.46	1.1	.697
My supervisor gives me adequate information about my job performance.	3.66	1.1	.695
I know exactly what my supervisor expects of me.	3.95	1.0	.681
I am dissatisfied with the way this institution is run.	2.62	1.1	.693
I would like to continue working at this institution.	4.18	.96	.626
I am satisfied with my co-workers.	3.87	.81	.521
I am satisfied with my supervisors.	3.78	.97	.759

Scale mean (SD): Private: 3.64 (.57) Public: 3.52 (.55)
Range: 1-5
Cronbach's alpha: 894
N: Private: 833 Public: 426

15. Support of Staff Scale	Mean	SD	Item to Total Correlation
Staff receive encouragement from supervisors to do their job well.	3.54	1.0	.776
Facility administration blame the staff when there is a problem.	3.01	1.1	.635
Supervisors handle problems with the staff in a friendly way.	3.52	.88	.760
Administrators handle problems with the staff in professional way.	3.69	.95	.787
The staff praise one another when they do their jobs well.	3.48	.92	.737
The staff support one another in the job of resident management.	3.81	.86	.747
The direct care staff work well with other staff members such as the teachers and counselors.	3.75	.83	.740
The direct care staff think the work of counselors and teachers is important.	3.93	.92	.716

Scale mean (SD): Private: 3.69 (.71) Public:3.54 (.68)
Range: 1-5
Cronbach's alpha: .880
N: Private: 834 Public: 430

16. Personal Stress Scale	Mean	SD	Item to Total Correlation
During the past 6 months,			
how often have you had a feeling of depression.	2.05	.94	.766
a feeling that nothing turns out right for you.	1.87	.84	.744
a feeling that nothing is worth while.	1.58	.76	.693
a disturbed or restless sleep.	2.27	1.0	.733
a concern that something is wrong with your body.	1.96	.92	.686
a feeling of tenseness or anxiety.	2.35	.97	.810
difficulty concentrating.	2.00	.83	.760
a feeling that you are worrying too much.	2.22	1.0	.781
a feeling that everything is going wrong.	1.76	.82	.761
personal worries that bothered you.	2.29	.89	.701
a feeling of being weak all over.	1.54	.74	.658
recurring headaches.	1.76	.95	.629
a feeling of frustration because of your job.	2.43	1.1	.758
a feeling of being very angry.	2.02	.90	.746
Scale mean (SD): Private: 1.97(.63) Public: 2.02 (.67)	Range: 1-5		
Cronbach's alpha: .932	N: Private: 832 Public: 427		

17. Staff Communication Scale	Mean	SD	Item to Total Correlation
Communications are effective between...			
upper level managers and the correctional officers.	3.33	.95	.840
upper level managers and the line supervisors.	3.50	.88	.857
line supervisors and the correctional officers.	3.56	.87	.860
treatment staff and the correctional officers.	3.49	.88	.845
The expected course of action for handling the residents is effectively communicated to the staff.	3.71	.91	.861
Policies and procedure for managing residents are communicated to the staff effectively.	3.71	.92	.870
Staff meetings or role calls are effective in communicating information necessary for managing the residents.	3.71	1.0	.807

Scale mean (SD): Private: 3.68 (.79) Public: 3.52 (.77)
Range: 1-5
Cronbach's alpha: .934
N: Private: 803 Public: 413

Appendix E: Facility Indices

1. Admission Process Index	Private	Public
	(% yes)	(% yes)
The court determines who is assigned to the facility.	62.5	40.6
A juvenile correctional agency determines who is assigned to the facility.	62.5	75
The personnel at this facility determine who is assigned to the facility.	43.8	31.3
Juveniles are interviewed by a facility staff member prior to admission into the facility.	50	43.8
Juveniles must volunteer to be considered for the facility.	12.5	12.5
Juveniles may voluntarily leave this program.	0	12.5
This facility admits juveniles with histories of abuse (either physical or sexual).	93.8	100
This facility admits juveniles evaluated as having psychological problems.	62.5	90.6
This facility admits juveniles evaluated as being suicide risks.	68.8	78.2
Juveniles must pass a physical evaluation prior to admission to the facility.	75	62.5
Juveniles must pass a medical evaluation prior to admission to the facility.	87.5	59.4
Juveniles must pass a psychological evaluation prior to admission to the facility.	68.8	50

Note: Items coded as: 0 = No, 1 = Yes

2. Population Seriousness Index	Private		Public	
	M	SD	M	SD
Do you accept the following types of juvenile delinquents?				
Juveniles waived to adult criminal court.	.19	.54	.44	.76
Adjudicated juveniles convicted of violent crimes.	1.56	.73	1.59	.71
Juveniles with a past history of engaging in violent acts.	1.56	.72	1.59	.76
Juveniles convicted of arson.	1.0	.89	1.22	.94
Juveniles convicted of sex offenses.	.94	.93	1.13	.98
Adjudicated juveniles previously convicted of serious offenses.	1.50	.82	1.75	.51
Status offenders.	.69	.87	.72	.92

Note: Items coded as: 0=No, 1=Limited number of admission, 2=Yes

References

Austin, J. (1998). *Debate on Privatization in Corrections: Against Privatization in Corrections.* Paper presented at the annual meeting of the American Society of Criminology, Washington, DC.

Bartollas, C. (1997). *Juvenile Delinquency* (4TH ed.). Boston, MA: Allyn and Bacon.

Bernard, T.J. (1992). *The Cycle of Juvenile Justice.* New York: Oxford University Press.

Blakely, C.R., & Bumphus, V.W. (1996). Private correctional management: A comparison of enabling legislation. *Federal Probation,* 60(2), 49-55.

Bonta, J., & Gendreau, P. (1988). Re-examining the cruel and unusual punishment of prison life. Unpublished manuscript.

Breed, A., & Krisberg, B. (1986). Is there a future? *Corrections Today,* 48, 14-26.

Butterfield, F. (1998, July 15). Profits at juvenile prisons are earned at a chilling cost. *New York Times,* p. A1.

Camp, C., & Camp, G. (1984). *Private Sector Involvement in Prison Services and Operations.* South Salem, NY: Criminal Justice Institute.

Clinton, T.W., Stolzenberg, L., & D'Alessio, S.J. (1997). Private versus public placement: A study of recidivism among adjudicated juvenile offenders. *Juvenile and Family Court Journal,* 48(3), 33-40.7

Comrey, A.L., & Lee, H.B. (1992). *A First Course in Factor Analysis* (2nd edition). Hillsdale, NJ: Lawrence Erlbaum Associates, Publishers.

Conway, M.R. (1990). A random effect model for binary data. *Biometrics,* 46, 317-328.

Cronbach, L. J. (1951). Coefficient alpha and the internal structure of tests. *Psychometrika,* 16, 397-334.

Demchak, T. (1989). Changes anticipated in Arizona and Arkansas juvenile facilities. *Youth Law News,* 10, 8-10.

Dickman, S.J. (1990). Functional and dysfunctional impulsivity: Personality and cognitive correlates. *Journal of Personality and Social Psychology,* 58(1), 95-102.

DiIulio, J.J.(1991).*No Escape: The Future of American Corrections.* New York,NY:Basic Books.

DiIulio, J.J. (1993). Rethinking the criminal justice system: Toward a new paradigm. *In Performance Measures for the Criminal Justice System.* U.S. Department of Justice, Office of Justice Programs, Bureau of Justice Statistics: Washington, DC.

DiIulio, J.J. (1988). What's wrong with private prisons? *Public Interest,* 92, 66-83.

DiPiano, J. (1991). Private Prisons: Can they work? Panopticon in the 21th century. *New England Journal on Criminal and Civil Confinement,* 21(1), 171-202.

Ethridge, P.A., & Marquart, J.W. (1993). Private prisons in Texas: The new penology for profit. *Justice Quarterly,* 10(1), 29-48.

Farbstein, J., & Wener, R. (1982). Evaluation of correctional environments. *Environment and Behavior*, 14, 671-694.

Feeley, M.M. (1991). Privatization of prisons in historical perspective. In W. Gormley (ed.), *Privatization and Its Alternatives*. Madison, WI: University of Wisconsin Press.

Flanagan, T.J. (1983). Correlates of institutional misconduct among state prisoners. *Criminology*, 21, 29-39.

Gendreau, P., & Goggin, C. (1997). Correctional treatment: Accomplishments and realities. In P. VanVoorhis, M. Braswell & D. Lester (Eds.), *Correctional Counseling and Rehabilitation*. Cincinnati, OH: Anderson.

Gendreau, P., & Andrews, D.A. (1994). *The Correctional Program Evaluation Inventory.* Unpublished Manuscript.

Goetting, A., & Howsen, R.M. (1986). Correlates of Prisoner Misconduct. *Journal of Quantitative Criminology,* 2(1), 49-67.

Goodstein, L., & Wright, K.N. (1989). Inmate adjustment to prison. In D.L. MacKenzie & L. Goodstein, *The American Prison: Issues in Research and Policy.* New York, NY: Plenum Press.

Gover, A.R., Styve, G.J., & MacKenzie, D.L.(2000, forthcoming). Importation and deprivation explanations of juveniles' adjustment to correctional facilities. *Journal of Criminal Justice.*

Harding, R.W. (1998). Private Prisons. In M. Tonry (Ed.) *The Handbook of Crime and Punishment.* New York: Oxford University Press.

Harding, R.W. (1997). *Private Prisons and Public Accountability.* New Brunswick, NJ: Transaction Publishers.

Harer, M., & Steffensmeier, D.(1996). Race and prison violence. *Criminology,* 34(3), 323-355.

Hatry, H.P., Brounstein, P.J., & Levinson, R.B.(1993).Comparison of privately and publicly operated corrections institutions in Kentucky and Massachusetts. In G.W. Bowman, S. Hakim, & P. Seidenstat(Eds.), *Privatizing Correctional Institutions.* New Brunswick, NJ: Transaction Publishers.

Hodges, M.C. (1997). *Information Brief: Comparing costs of public and private prisons.* Tallahassee, FL: Florida Office of Program Policy Analysis and Government Accountability.

Howell, J.C., Krisberg, B., Hawkins, J.D., & Wilson, J.J. (1995). *Serious, Violent, & Chronic Juvenile Offenders.* Thousand Oaks, CA: Sage.

Irwin, J., & Cressey, D. (1962). Thieves, convicts, and the inmate culture. *Social Problems,* 10, 142-155.

Jablonski, J.R.(1991).*Implementing Total Quality Management: An Overview.* San Diego: Pfeiffer.

Jacobs, J.B. (1976). Stratification and conflict among prison inmates. *Journal of Criminal Law and Criminology*, 66, 476-482.

Jaman, D.R., Coburn, P., Goddard, J., & Mueller, F.C. (1966). *Characteristics of Violent Prisoners.* Sacramento, CA: California Department of Corrections.

Jan, L. (1980). Overcrowding and inmate behavior: Some preliminary findings. *Criminal Justice and Behavior,* 7, 293-301.

Jensen, G.F. (1977). Age and rule-breaking in prison. *Criminology,* 14, 555-568.

Jessness, C.F.(1962).*Jessness Inventory.* North Tonawanda, NY: Multi Health Systems.

Knight, K.M., Holcom, M., & Simpson, D.D. (1994). *TCU Psychosocial Functioning and Motivation Scales: Manual on Psychometric Properties.* Institute of Behavioral Research. Fort Worth, TX: Texas Christian University Press.

Krisberg, B. (1995). The legacy of juvenile corrections. *Corrections Today*, 57, 122-154.

Krisberg, B., Schwartz, I., Fishman, G., Eisikovits, Z., & Guttman, E.(1986).*The Imprisonment of Minority Youth.* Minneapolis,MN: Hubert H. Humphries Institute of Public Administration.

Lanza-Kaduce, L., Parker, K.F., & Thomas, C. (1999). A comparative recidivism analysis of releasees from private and public prisons in Florida. *Crime and Delinquency,* 45, 28-47.

Lawson, D., Segrin, C., & Ward, T. (1996). Relationship between prisonization and social skills among prison inmates. *The Prison Journal,* 76(3), 293-309.

Levinson, R.B., & Taylor, W.J. (1991). ACA studies privatization in juvenile corrections. *Corrections Today*, 53, 242-248.

Logan, C.H. (1999). Www.ucc.uconn.edu/~wwwsoci/prismeas.html.

Logan, C.H. (1992). Well kept: Comparing quality of confinement in private and public prisons. *The Journal of Criminal Law and Criminology,* 8(3), 577-613.

Logan, C. H. (1990). *Private Prisons: Pros and Cons.* New York: Oxford University Press.

MacDonald, J. (1999). Violence and juvenile drug use in juvenile institutions. *Journal of Criminal Justice,* 27(1), 33-44.

MacKenzie, D.L., (1987). Age and adjustment to prison: Interactions with attitudes and anxiety. *Criminal Justice and Behavior,* 14(4), 427-447.

MacKenzie, D.L., Styve, G.J., & Gover, A.R. (1998). Performance-based standards for juvenile corrections. *Corrections Management Quarterly,* 2(2), 28-35.

Maxwell, S.E., & Delaney, H.D. (1990). *Designing Experiments and Analyzing Data: A Model Comparison Perspective.* Belmont, CA: Wadsworth Publishing Co.

McDonald, D.C. (1990). *Private Prisons and the Public Interest.* New Brunswick, NJ: Rutgers University Press.

McKelvey, B. (1977). *American Prisons* (2nd edition). Montclair, NJ: Patterson Smith.

Medina v. O'Neill 589 F. Supp. 1028 (1984).

Mitchell, O., MacKenzie, D., Gover, A., & Styve, G. (1999). The environment and working conditions in juvenile boot camps and traditional facilities. *Justice Research and Policy,* 1(2).

Moos,R.H.(1975).*Evaluating Correctional and Community Settings.* New York: Macmillan Press.

Moos, R.H. (1974). *Correctional Institutions Environment Scale Manual.* Palo Alto, CA: Consulting Psychological Press.

Moos, R. H. (1971). Differential effects of the social climates of correctional institutions. *Journal of Research in Crime and Delinquency,* 7, 71-82.

Myers, L.B., & Levy, G.W. (1978). Description and prediction of the intractable inmate. *Journal of Research in Crime and Delinquency,* 15, 214-228.

Ogle, R.(1999). Prison Privatization: An Environmental Catch-22. *Justice Quarterly,*16(3),579-600.

Osborne, D., & Gaebler, T. (1982). *Reinventing Government.* New York: Prager.

Ott, L. (1988). *An Introduction to Statistical Methods and Data Analysis* (3rd edition). Boston: PWS-Kent Publishing Company.

Parisi, N. (1982). The prisoner's pressures and responses. In N. Parisi (Ed.), *Coping with Imprisonment: Perspectives in Criminal Justice.* Beverly Hills, CA: Sage.

Paulus, P.B., McCain, G., & Cox, V.C. (1978). Death rates, psychiatric commitments, blood pressure and perceived crowding as a function of institutional crowding. *Environmental Psychology and Nonverbal Behavior,* 3, 107-116.

Petersilia, J. (1993). Measuring the performance of community corrections. In *Performance Measures for the Criminal Justice System.* Bureau of Justice Statistics and Princeton University: U.S. Department of Justice.

Petersilia, J., & Honing, P. (1980). *The Prison Experience of Career Criminals.* Santa Monica,CA: Rand Corporation.

Porporino, F.J., & Zamble, E. (1984). Coping with imprisonment. *Canadian Journal of Criminology,* 26(4), 403-422.

Pratt, T.C., & Maahs, J. (1999). Are private prisons more cost-effective than public prisons? A meta-analysis of evaluation research studies. *Crime and Delinquency,* 45(3), 358-371.

Robbins, I.P. (1986). Privatization of corrections: Defining the issues. *Federal Probation,* 50, 24-30.

Ryan, M. (1993). Evaluating and responding to private prisons in the United Kingdom. *International Journal of the Sociology of Law,* 21, 319-333.

Scott, W.R. (1992). *Organizations: Rational, Natural and Open Systems* (2nd edition). Englewood Cliffs, NJ: Prentice Hall.

Shichor, D., & Sechrest, D.K. (1995). Quick fixes in corrections:. Reconsidering private and public for-profit institutions. *The Prison Journal,* 75(4), 457478

Shichor, D., & Bartollas, C. (1990). Private and public juvenile placements: Is there a difference? *Crime and Delinquency,* 36(2), 286-299.

Siegel, L., & Senna, J. (1996). *Juvenile Delinquency: Theory, Practice and Law* (6th edition). St. Paul, MN: West Publishing Company.

Spielberger, C.D., Gorsuch, R.L., & Lushene, R.E. (1970). *Manual for the State-Trait Anxiety Inventory.* Palo Alto, CA: Consulting Psychologists Press.

Stojkovic, S. (1984). Social bases of power and control mechanisms among prisoners in a prison organization. *Justice Quarterly,* 1(1), 511-528.

Styve, G., MacKenzie, D., Gover, A., & Mitchell, O. (2000). Perceived conditions of confinement: A national evaluation of juvenile boot camps and traditional facilities. *Law and Human Behavior,* 24(3), 1-25.

Sykes, G.M. (1958). *The Society of Captives.* Princeton, NJ: Princeton University Press.

Sykes, G.M., & Messinger, S.L.(1960). The inmate social system. In G. Grosser (ed.), *Theoretical Studies in Social Organization of the Prison.* New York: Social Science Research Council.

Thomas, C. (1999). Www.privatemanagement.com.

Thomas, C., & Bolinger, T. (July, 1996). Private adult correctional facility census: Statistical highlights for 1995. *Corrections Compendium,* 20-23.
Toch, H. (1977). *Living in Prison: The Ecology of Survival.* New York: McMillan.

U.S. Department of Justice, Bureau of Justice Statistics (August, 1999). *Prisoners in 1998.* Washington, D.C.: Government Printing Office.

U.S. Department of Justice, Bureau of Justice Statistics (August, 1997). *Prisoners in 1996.* Washington, D.C.: Government Printing Office.

U.S. Department of Justice, Office of Juvenile Justice and Delinquency Prevention (1999). *1997 Children in Custody Census.* Washington, D.C.: Government Printing Office.

U.S. Department of Justice (1999). *1997 Census of Juveniles in Residential Placement.* Washington, D.C.: Government Printing Office.

U.S. Department of Justice, Office of Juvenile Justice and Delinquency Prevention (1997). *Juveniles in Private Institutions 1991-1995.* Washington, D.C.: Government Printing Office.

U.S. Department of Justice, Office of Juvenile Justice and Delinquency Prevention (1994). *Conditions of Confinement: Juvenile Detention and Correctional Institutions.* Washington, D.C.: Government Printing Office.

U.S. Department of Justice, Federal Bureau of Prisons (1993). *Prison Social Climate Survey: Staff Version and Resident Version.* Washington, D.C.: Government Printing Office.

U.S. General Accounting Office (1991). *Private Prisons.* Washington, D.C.: Government Printing Office.

U.S. Department of Justice (1986). *Historical Corrections Statistics in the United States, 1850-1984.* Washington, D.C.: Government Printing Office.

Winn, R.G. (1996). Ideology and the calculation of efficiency in public and private correctional enterprise. In G.L. Mays & T. Gray (Eds.) *Privatization and the Provision of Correctional Services: Context and Consequences.* Cincinnati, OH: Anderson.

Wolfgang, M.E., (1961). Quantitative analysis of adjustment to the prison community. *Journal of Criminal Law, Criminology & Police Science,* 51, 608-618.

Wordes, M., & Jones, S.M. (1998). Trends in juvenile detention and steps toward reform. *Crime and Delinquency,* 44(4), 544-560.

Wright, K.N. (1991). A study of individual, environmental, and interactive effects in explaining adjustment to prison. *Justice Quarterly, 8*(2), 217-242.

Wright, K.N. (1985). Developing the Prison Environment Inventory. *Journal of Research in Crime and Delinquency,* 22(3), 257-277.

Wright,K.N.(1983).Prison environment and behavioral outcomes. *Journal of Offender Rehabilitation,*20,93-113.

Wright, K.N., & Boudouris, J. (1982). An assessment of the Moos Correctional Institutions Environment Scale. *Journal of Research in Crime and Delinquency,* 19, 255-27

INDEX

Printed in the United States
27926LVS00001BA/3